SAS® Guide to the SQL Procedure: Usage and Reference

Version 6
First Edition

SAS Institute Inc.
SAS Campus Drive
Cary, NC 27513

The correct bibliographic citation for this manual is as follows: SAS Institute Inc., *SAS® Guide to the SQL Procedure: Usage and Reference, Version 6, First Edition*, Cary, NC: SAS Institute Inc., 1989, 210 pp.

SAS® Guide to the SQL Procedure: Usage and Reference, Version 6, First Edition

Contents

Reference Aids   vii

Credits   ix

Using This Book   xi

Part 1 · Introduction   1

Chapter 1 · Introduction to the SQL Procedure   3

Introduction   3

Basic Concepts and Terms   3

The SQL Procedure of the Base SAS System   5

Chapter Summary   8

Part 2 · Usage Guide for the SQL Procedure   9

Chapter 2 · Retrieving Data with the SELECT Statement   11

Introduction   11

Querying a Single Table   12

Specifying Rows with the WHERE Clause   19

Specifying Rows with a HAVING Expression   23

Querying Multiple Tables   24

Using Subqueries   31

When to Use Joins and Subqueries   35

Using the VALIDATE Statement   36

Chapter Summary   37

Chapter 3 · Creating and Modifying Tables and Views   39

Introduction   39

Creating a Table   40

Creating and Using a View Definition   42

Creating and Using an Index   49

Modifying a Table and Its Data   50

Resetting SQL Procedure Options   57

Chapter Summary   58

Chapter 4 · Using the Advanced Features of the SQL Procedure 59

Introduction 59

Advanced Features of the SQL Procedure 59

Improving Query Performance 74

SQL Procedure with Other SAS Interfaces 78

Chapter Summary 83

Part 3 · Reference Guide for the SQL Procedure 85

Chapter 5 · SQL Procedure 87

Overview 88

Syntax 88

Statements in the SQL Procedure 95

Macro Variables Set by Statements in the SQL Procedure 118

Components of the SQL Procedure Statements 120

Chapter Summary 181

Part 4 · Appendices 183

Appendix 1 · Sample Tables 185

Introduction 185

Employee Table 185

Customer Table 186

Product Table 187

Invoice Table 187

Appendix 2 · SQL Procedure and the ANSI Standard for SQL 189

Introduction 189

SQL Procedure Enhancements 190

SQL Procedure Omissions 192

Glossary 195

Bibliography 201

Index 203

In this book, brief messages that are written to the SAS log begin with the words NOTE, ERROR, or WARNING. Here is an example:

```
NOTE:  Table WORK.TEST modified, with 2 columns.
```

Additional Documentation

There are many SAS System publications available. To receive a free *Publications Catalog*, write, call, or fax the Institute (or access the online version of the *Publications Catalog* via the World Wide Web):

> SAS Institute Inc.
> Book Sales Department
> SAS Campus Drive
> Cary, NC 27513
> Telephone: 919-677-8000 - then press 1-7001
> Fax: 919-677-4444
> Email: sasbook@unx.sas.com
> WWW: http://www.sas.com/

☐ *Getting Started with the SQL Procedure, Version 6, First Edition* (order #A55042) uses examples that show you how to program with the SQL procedure.

☐ *SAS Guide to the SQL Query Window: Usage and Reference, Version 6, First Edition* (order #A55342) uses examples that show you how to use this point-and-click interface to the SQL procedure.

☐ *SAS Language and Procedures: Introduction, Version 6, First Edition* (order #A56074) gets you started if you are unfamiliar with the SAS System or any programming language.

☐ *SAS Language and Procedures: Usage, Version 6, First Edition* (order #A56075) and *SAS Language and Procedures: Usage 2, Version 6, First Edition* (order #A56078) are user's guides to the SAS System. They show you how to use base SAS software for data analysis, report writing, and data manipulation.

☐ *SAS Language: Reference, Version 6, First Edition* (#A56076) provides detailed information on base SAS software, the SAS programming language, and the types of applications the SAS System can perform.

☐ SAS Technical Report P-222, *Changes and Enhancements to Base SAS Software, Release 6.07* (order #A59139) provides the latest features and changes to Release 6.07 base SAS software, including enhancements to the SQL procedure.

☐ *SAS Procedures Guide, Version 6, Third Edition* (order #A56080) provides detailed information about the procedures available in the SAS System.

☐ *SAS Screen Control Language: Usage, Version 6, First Edition* (order #A56031) shows you how to write SCL programs.

☐ *SAS Guide to Macro Processing, Version 6, Second Edition* (order #A56041) describes the macro facility in base SAS software that can be used with the SQL procedure.

☐ The Version 6 edition of the SAS companion for your operating environment provides information about the specific features of the SAS System under your environment.

SAS/ACCESS Documentation

☐ *Getting Started with SAS/ACCESS Software, Version 6, First Edition* (order #A55103) uses tutorials to show you how to create and edit access descriptors and view descriptors. It also shows you how to insert data into a database table and how to use the SQL Procedure Pass-Through facility.

☐ *SAS/ACCESS Software for Relational Databases: Reference, Version 6, First Edition* (order #A55144) provides general information for all of the relational database management systems (DBMSs) that can be used with SAS/ACCESS software. This book must be used with one or more of the DBMS chapters below.

    ☐ *AS/400 Data Chapter, Version 6, First Edition* (order #A55155)

    ☐ *DB2 Chapter, Version 6, Second Edition* (order #A55470)

    ☐ *DB2/2 Chapter, Version 6, First Edition* (order #A55142)*

    ☐ *DEC Rdb Chapter, Version 6, First Edition* (order #A55161) **

    ☐ *INGRES Chapter, Version 6, First Edition* (order #A55133)

    ☐ *ORACLE Chapter, Version 6, First Edition* (order #A55226)

    ☐ *SQL/DS Chapter, Version 6, Second Edition* (order #A55471)

    ☐ *SYBASE and SQL Server Chapter, Version 6, First Edition* (order #A55310)

☐ *SAS/ACCESS Software Changes and Enhancements: SQL Procedure Pass-Through Facility, Version 6* (order #A55237) describes SAS/ACCESS interfaces that are available only with the Pass-Through facility. This report applies to the following DBMSs: DB2 for UNIX, Informix (under UNIX environments), ODBC—drivers that conform to the open database connectivity standards (under OS/2, Microsoft Windows and Windows NT), ORACLE (Alpha OSF), and SYBASE and SQL Server (under OpenVMS). These last two interfaces also run under certain MIPS ABI- and Intel ABI-compliant machines.

☐ *SAS/ACCESS Interface to ADABAS: Usage and Reference, Version 6, First Edition* (order #A56065)

☐ *SAS/ACCESS Interface to CA-DATACOM/DB: Usage and Reference, Version 6, First Edition* (order #A56066)

☐ *SAS/ACCESS Interface to CA-IDMS: Usage and Reference, Version 6, First Edition* (order #A55180)

☐ *SAS/ACCESS Interface to IMS-DL/I: Usage and Reference, Version 6, Second Edition* (order #A55270)

☐ *SAS/ACCESS Software for PC File Formats: Reference, Version 6, First Edition* (order #A55206) provides general information for all of the PC file formats that can be used with SAS/ACCESS software. It contains PC format-specific chapters for DBF, DIF, WK*n* and XLS files. This book comes in a loose-leaf binder so that you can update it easily as new file formats become available.

☐ *SAS/ACCESS Interface to SYSTEM 2000 Data Management Software: Usage and Reference, Version 6, First Edition* (order #A56064)

---

* IBM has renamed its OS/2 Database Manager product to Database 2 OS/2, or DB2/2 for short.

** Digital Equipment Corp. has renamed its Rdb/VMS product to DEC Rdb.

Credits

Documentation

Composition	Gail C. Freeman, Cynthia Hopkins, Pamela A. Troutman, David S. Tyree
Illustrations	Laura B. Hill, Ginny Matsey
Proofreading	Beth A. Heiney, Beryl C. Pittman, Josephine P. Pope, Toni P. Sherrill, Michael H. Smith, John M. West, Susan E. Willard
Technical Review	Eric C. Brinsfield, Lewis Church, Jr., Leslie B. Clinton, Anne Corrigan, Henrietta H. Cummings, Ginny Dineley, Tom C. Edds, Paul M. Kent, Mark E. Stranieri
Writing and Editing	Catherine C. Carter, Susan E. Johnston, Kathryn A. Restivo

Software

Product development includes design, programming, debugging, support, and preliminary documentation. In the following list, developers who currently support the procedure or features are indicated with an asterisk. Others provided specific assistance for this release or assisted in the development of the procedure or features in previous releases.

Development Testing Support	Leslie B. Clinton*
Quality Assurance Testing	Mark E. Stranieri
SQL Research Prototype	Paul M. Kent*, Jeffrey A. Polzin, Jack J. Rouse, John P. Sall
Version 6 SQL Implementation	Lewis Church, Jr.*, Henrietta H. Cummings*, Paul M. Kent*

x

Using This Book

Purpose

SAS Guide to the SQL Procedure: Usage and Reference, Version 6, First Edition provides both tutorial and reference information on the SQL procedure. The SQL procedure implements the Structured Query Language (SQL™) in the SAS System, beginning with Release 6.06.

The two types of information are presented in separate parts of this book. The usage (or tutorial) portion introduces the most frequently used SQL procedure statements and explains how these can be used to process your data. It does not, however, attempt to cover all the components or tasks that you can accomplish with the procedure. The reference portion provides complete descriptions of all the options, statements, and components that make up the SQL procedure, but it does not attempt to teach you how to use the procedure.

This section explains how you can best use this book. Each part of the book is described so that you know where to go based on your level of knowledge and experience with SQL. See "Additional Documentation" later in "Using This Book" for other SAS publications that may provide useful information.

Audience

This book is intended for application programmers and end users who are knowledgeable about the SAS System and their own operating systems. No knowledge of SQL or relational databases is assumed, although some users may be familiar with them.

Prerequisites

This book assumes you are familiar with basic SAS System concepts. See the following table for more information on the concepts you need to know in order to use the SQL procedure.

SQL is a trademark of International Business Machines Corporation.

You need to know how to	Refer to
use your host operating system	vendor's documentation for your host system and the Version 6 SAS documentation for your host system
invoke the SAS System at your site	check with the SAS Software Consultant at your site
reference files in SAS data libraries and assign librefs use the SAS text editor to enter and edit text	*SAS Language and Procedures: Usage, Version 6, First Edition*
manipulate SAS data sets beginning with Release 6.06 use the SAS text editor to enter and edit text (advanced information)	*SAS Language: Reference, Version 6, First Edition*

If you have not used Version 6 of the SAS System, you should refer to *SAS Language: Reference, Version 6, First Edition* for information on how SAS data sets are implemented beginning with Release 6.06.

For more information on the SAS System, see "Additional Documentation" later in this section.

How to Use This Book

This section gives you an overview of the book's organization and content. The book's parts and the chapters they include are described, followed by a section on how to use each chapter.

Organization

SAS Guide to the SQL Procedure: Usage and Reference is divided into four parts.

Part 1: Introduction

Part 1 contains an introduction to SQL and the SQL procedure. It shows you how the SQL procedure works in the SAS System and how you use PROC SQL views in other SAS procedures. PROC SQL's operations and abilities are also compared with the DATA step and other SAS procedures.

Chapter 1, "Introduction to the SQL Procedure"

Part 2: Usage Guide to the SQL Procedure

Part 2 makes up a tutorial and usage guide to the SQL procedure. These chapters are composed of examples that range from the simple to the complex, each giving a step-by-step introduction to the SQL statements and their clauses and components.

Chapter 2, "Retrieving Data with the SELECT Statement"

Chapter 3, "Creating and Modifying Tables and Views"

Chapter 4, "Using the Advanced Features of the SQL Procedure"

Part 3: Reference Guide to the SQL Procedure

Part 3 serves as a reference guide to the SQL procedure. It describes the SQL procedure's options, statements, and components. It explains how the procedure works and what you can accomplish with it.

Chapter 5, "SQL Procedure"

Part 4: Appendices

Part 4 contains two appendices. Appendix 1 contains the sample tables used in most of this book's examples. Appendix 2 lists the enhancements that SAS Institute has made to the Structured Query Language through the SQL procedure and ways in which the procedure has omitted certain features described in the American National Standards Institute (ANSI) guidelines.

Appendix 1, "Sample Tables"

Appendix 2, "SQL Procedure and the ANSI Standard for SQL"

What You Should Read

This book is written for several types of users. If you are unfamiliar with the SAS System, you can refer to "Additional Documentation" later in this section. Users and their knowledge levels are summarized as follows:

If you are	You should read
an end user who is familiar with the SAS System but who has no previous experience with SQL	Chapters 1 through 3 and Appendix 1. Once you feel adept with them, read Chapter 5 and then Chapter 4.
an applications programmer who is familiar with the SAS System and who has some experience with SQL	Chapters 1 through 3 and Appendix 1. Once you feel adept with that information, read Chapter 5.
an applications programmer who is familiar with the SAS System and who has extensive experience with SQL	Chapters 1 through 3 and Appendix 1 briefly. Concentrate on Chapters 4 and 5. Review Appendix 2 to compare the SQL procedure with the ANSI Standard for SQL.

Reference Aids

The following features of this book are provided for your easy reference:

Glossary	contains commonly used SQL and SAS terms and concepts.
Bibliography	includes books and periodicals on SQL and relational database theory and practice.
Index	references all pertinent terms and concepts.

Conventions

This section covers the conventions this book uses, including typographical conventions, syntax conventions, and conventions used in presenting output.

Typographical Conventions

This book uses several type styles. Style conventions are summarized here:

roman	is the basic type style used for most text.
UPPERCASE ROMAN	is used for references in the text to keywords of SQL and the SAS language, to column names, and to excerpts of code.
italic	is used for terms that are defined in the Glossary and to stress or emphasize important information.
`monospace`	is used to show examples of programming code (both SAS and SQL statements). In most cases, this book uses lowercase type for SAS code, with the exception of some title characters. You can enter your own code in lowercase, uppercase, or a mixture of the two. The SAS System always changes your column names to uppercase, but character values remain in lowercase if you have entered them that way. Enter any titles and footnotes exactly as you want them to appear on your output.

Syntax Conventions

Syntax conventions are used to show the basic format of a SAS statement. This book uses the following conventions for syntax:

UPPERCASE BOLD	indicates a SAS keyword or the names of statements and clauses in the SQL procedure. You should use the same spelling as shown, although the SAS System is not case-sensitive.
UPPERCASE ROMAN	indicates SQL keywords or statement options whose values have the exact spelling and form shown. They may or may not be optional, depending on whether they are enclosed in angle brackets ($<>$). Note that you do not have to use uppercase when you type keywords or options.
lowercase roman	indicates the name of a component in the SQL procedure. Each component is described separately in Chapter 5. A component may or may not be optional, depending on whether it is enclosed in angle brackets ($<>$).
italic	indicates items in statement syntax (arguments) for which you supply a value.
<arguments in angle brackets>	are optional. A comma is often used to separate arguments.
multiple arguments within one set of angle brackets	means that if you use one argument, you must use all the arguments.
arguments not in angle brackets	are required.
| (vertical bar)	means that you can choose only one of the components, keywords, or options from a group. If all the components, keywords, or options are enclosed in angle brackets, the entire list is optional.
. . . (ellipsis)	means that the parameter (or set of parameters enclosed in angle brackets) immediately preceding the ellipsis can be repeated.
; (semicolon)	indicates the end of a SAS statement. Every SAS statement must end with a semicolon.

The following example illustrates these syntax conventions:

PROC SQL <STIMER <NUMBER>...>;
SELECT object-item <,object-item <column-modifier>...>...
    FROM *libref.view-name* <<AS> *alias*> <, table-name>...
    <**ORDER BY***constant* <, object-item>...>;

PROC SQL, SELECT, FROM, ORDER BY
> are primary parts of SQL so they appear in bold type. PROC SQL is the procedure's name, SELECT is one of its statements, and FROM and ORDER BY are clauses within the SELECT statement.

STIMER, NUMBER
> are options specific to a SAS PROC statement. You can use the PROC SQL statement with any number of options, or no options. Options are separated with a blank space. The options are in uppercase to indicate that they must be spelled as shown.

libref.view-name <<AS> *alias*>
> means that you substitute a value for the italicized argument. The argument is followed by an optional argument that can be specified with an optional SQL keyword (in this case, AS). The keyword is a literal.

object-item
> refers to the name of a component in the SQL procedure that is described fully in Chapter 5, following the statement descriptions. A component can contain other components and SQL keywords.

<, object-item <column-modifier>...>...
> indicates optionally specified multiple object-items (that is, components) that can be followed optionally by one or more components (or arguments). A comma is often used to separate components.

Conventions for Examples and Output

The examples in this book show you how to combine PROC SQL statements and options to achieve the results you want. You can run any of the examples in this book as you read the chapters. Examples are included in the member SQLUGDAT of the SAS System Sample Library. Most examples use permanent SAS data sets because several examples in a chapter or part may use the same data set.

Each page of output produced by a procedure is enclosed in a box. Most of the programs in this book were run using the following SAS system options:

PAGESIZE=60   sets the length of the page to 60 lines.

LINESIZE=80   sets the length of the text line to 80 characters.

NONEWS   indicates you do not want installation-maintained news information to appear in your output.

NODATE   indicates you do not want the date and time to appear in your output.

In this book, brief messages that are written to the SAS log begin with the words NOTE, ERROR, or WARNING. Here is an example:

```
NOTE:  Table WORK.TEST modified, with 2 columns.
```

Additional Documentation

There are many SAS System publications available. To receive a free *Publications Catalog*, write to the following address:

> SAS Institute Inc.
> Book Sales Department
> SAS Campus Drive
> Cary, NC 27513

The following is a selected list of SAS publications that may be helpful to you.

☐ *SAS Language: Reference, Version 6, First Edition* (#A56076) provides detailed information on base SAS software, the SAS programming language, and the types of applications the SAS System can perform. Chapter 6, "SAS Files," explains how the implementation of SAS data sets has changed in Version 6 of the SAS System.

☐ *SAS Language and Procedures: Usage, Version 6, First Edition* (#A56075) is a user's guide to the SAS System. It shows you how to use base SAS software for data analysis, report writing, and data manipulation. It also includes information on modes of execution and the LIBNAME statement.

☐ *SAS Language and Procedures: Usage 2, Version 6, First Edition* (order #A56078) is a task-oriented usage guide that presents base SAS software features and procedures and shows users how to use the software to perform tasks of moderate difficulty. This guide is written for experienced SAS users who want help with specific tasks. It builds on the concepts and tasks presented in *SAS Language and Procedures: Usage, Version 6, First Edition*.

☐ *SAS Procedures Guide, Version 6, Third Edition* (order #A56080) provides detailed information about the procedures available in the SAS System.

☐ SAS Technical Report P-221, *SAS/ACCESS Software: Changes and Enhancements, Release 6.07* (order #A59138) describes new features and changes to Release 6.07 of the following SAS/ACCESS Interfaces: ADABAS, CA-DATACOM/DB, DB2, ORACLE, Rdb/VMS, SQL/DS, and SYSTEM 2000. It also provides information on the SQL Procedure Pass-Through facility for the following interfaces: DB2, ORACLE, Rdb/VMS, and SQL/DS.

☐ SAS Technical Report P-222, *Changes and Enhancements to Base SAS Software, Release 6.07* (order #P59139) provides the latest features and changes to Release 6.07 of base SAS software. It includes information on the new SAS system passwords and updating information for the SQL procedure.

□ The following interface guides explain how to use the SAS/ACCESS software with other software vendors' products. They explain how to create SAS/ACCESS descriptor files and provide more information on using them in SAS programs. For a complete list of SAS/ACCESS interface guides, consult the *Publications Catalog.*

　□ *SAS/ACCESS Interface to AS/400 Data: Usage and Reference, Version 6, First Edition* (order #A56073)

　□ *SAS/ACCESS Interface to DB2: Usage and Reference, Version 6, First Edition* (#A56060)

　□ *SAS/ACCESS Interface to INGRES: Usage and Reference, Version 6, First Edition* (order #A56072)

　□ *SAS/ACCESS Interface to ORACLE: Usage and Reference, Version 6, First Edition* (#A56061)

　□ *SAS/ACCESS Interface to ORACLE: Usage and Reference, Version 6, Second Edition* (order #A56082)

　□ *SAS/ACCESS Interface to OS/2 Database Manager: Usage and Reference, Version 6, First Edition* (order #A56071)

　□ *SAS/ACCESS Interface to PC File Formats: Usage and Reference, Version 6, First Edition* (order #A56079)

　□ *SAS/ACCESS Interface to Rdb/VMS: Usage and Reference, Version 6, First Edition* (#A56062)

　□ *SAS/ACCESS Interface to SQL/DS: Usage and Reference, Version 6, First Edition* (#A56063)

　□ *SAS/ACCESS Interface to SYBASE and SQL Server: Usage and Reference, Version 6, First Edition* (order #A56081)

　□ *SAS/ACCESS Interface to SYSTEM 2000 Data Management Software: Usage and Reference, Version 6, First Edition* (#A56064)

□ *SAS Screen Control Language: Reference, Version 6, First Edition* (#A56030) describes the Screen Control Language (SCL) interface that can be used with the SQL procedure. SCL is a programming language that provides functions and routines to control fields on a screen and to manage the screens that make up an application.

□ *SAS Guide to Macro Processing, Version 6 Edition* (#A5641) describes the macro facility in base SAS software that can be used with the SQL procedure. The macro facility is a programming tool for extending and customizing SAS software and for reducing the amount of text required to do common tasks.

□ The Version 6 edition of the SAS companion or other SAS documentation for your operating system provides information about the specific features of the SAS System under your operating system.

Part 1
Introduction

Chapter 1   **Introduction to the SQL Procedure**

Chapter 1 Introduction to the SQL Procedure

Introduction 3

Basic Concepts and Terms 3

The SQL Procedure of the Base SAS System 5
Comparing the SQL Procedure with the SAS DATA Step and Other SAS
 Procedures 6
Using PROC SQL Views in SAS Procedures 7

Chapter Summary 8

Introduction

This chapter describes the SQL procedure in Release 6.06 of the SAS System, which implements the Structured Query Language (SQL). It gives an overview of SQL, its history, and how it works within the SAS System. It also compares the SQL procedure with the SAS DATA step and other SAS procedures.

Basic Concepts and Terms

The Structured Query Language (SQL) is a standardized, widely used language that retrieves and updates data in relational tables and databases.

A relation is a mathematical concept that is similar to the mathematical concept of a set. Relations are represented physically as two-dimensional tables arranged in rows and columns. Relational theory was originally developed by E. F. Codd, an IBM® researcher, and first implemented at IBM in a prototype product called System R. This prototype later evolved into commercial IBM products based on SQL. The Structured Query Language is now in the public domain and is part of many vendors' products.

It is not necessary for users of the SQL procedure to study relational theory. An understanding of tables and their operations is the only requirement for using the SQL procedure within the SAS System. However, studying some elements of relational theory, such as normal forms, helps in designing tables and more efficient queries on those tables. See "Bibliography" later in this book for a list of books and periodicals on SQL and relational databases.

IBM is a registered trademark of International Business Machines Corporation.

The SAS System's SQL procedure gives you control over your data on three levels:

□ You can use the SELECT statement to retrieve data stored in tables or data accessed by PROC SQL or SAS/ACCESS views. (The SAS data files created by PROC SQL are referred to as tables in this book.) Or, you can use the VALIDATE statement to check the accuracy of your SELECT statement's syntax without actually executing it. You can also simply display a PROC SQL view definition in the SAS log using the DESCRIBE statement.

□ You can create tables, views, and indexes on columns in tables using the CREATE statement; these tables and views can be stored permanently in SAS data libraries and referred to with librefs. Or, you can delete tables, views, and indexes using the DROP statement.

□ You can add or modify the data values in a table's columns using the UPDATE statement or insert and delete rows with the INSERT and DELETE statements. You can use these same statements to update the data in an external database management system's (DBMS) tables and views that are described to the SAS System using SAS/ACCESS views. You can also modify a PROC SQL table itself by adding, modifying, or dropping columns with the ALTER statement.

The PROC SQL statement can also take a number of options, which can be added, changed, or removed when you use the RESET statement.

Figure 1.1 shows a table that describes employees in a sample beach-supplies wholesale company. Each *row* of the table gives information pertaining to one employee. Each *column* of the table describes a category of information about an employee, such as an employee number or job title.

Figure 1.1
Employee Table

column

EMPNUM	EMPNAME	EMPYEARS	EMPCITY	EMPTITLE	EMPBOSS
101	Herb	28	Ocean City	president	.
201	Betty	8	Ocean City	manager	101
213	Joe	2	Virginia Beach	salesrep	201
214	Jeff	1	Virginia Beach	salesrep	201
215	Wanda	10	Ocean City	salesrep	201
216	Fred	6	Ocean City	salesrep	201
301	Sally	9	Wilmington	manager	101
314	Marvin	5	Wilmington	salesrep	301
318	Nick	1	Myrtle Beach	salesrep	301
401	Chuck	12	Charleston	manager	101
417	Sam	7	Charleston	salesrep	401

row

The structure of tables is very similar to the structure of SAS data files.* SQL tables consist of rows and columns. In a SAS data file, the rows correspond to observations and the columns correspond to variables. SAS data files have an

---

* In Version 6 of the SAS System, a SAS data file is one of two implementations of a SAS data set. A SAS data file contains both data values and descriptor information. See Chapter 6, "SAS Files," in *SAS Language: Reference, Version 6, First Edition* for more information on SAS data sets and data files.

inherent ordering and concept of an *nth* observation; for example, you can specify a FIRST.*by-variable* and LAST.*by-variable* in a data file. An SQL table has no inherent or implied ordering. Otherwise, a SAS data file and an SQL table are so nearly identical that, in the SAS System, **a table is a SAS data file.** See Table 1.1 for a cross reference of equivalent terms used with SQL, the SAS System, and traditional data processing.

Table 1.1
Comparing
Equivalent Terms

SQL Term	Base SAS Term	Data Processing Term
table	SAS data file	file
row	observation	record
column	variable	field

SQL can be used in the SAS System in two ways. As a SAS procedure, the SQL procedure can process SQL statements in a SAS program or interactive session. Or, it can process SAS data files and SAS/ACCESS views created outside of PROC SQL. Other SAS procedures can read PROC SQL views or can read and update tables created through the SQL procedure. The DATA step can use a table as it would any SAS data file, or it can use PROC SQL views as input, for example, in the SET statement. The remainder of this book explains how to use the SQL procedure.

The SQL Procedure of the Base SAS System

The SQL procedure processes SQL statements that read and update tables. The PROC SQL SELECT statement in the next example retrieves and displays the name, city, and service years for sales representatives in the Employee table:

```
proc sql;
title 'City and Years of Service';
select empname, empcity, empyears
   from sql.employee
   where emptitle='salesrep';
```

```
                    City and Years of Service                    1

            EMPNAME   EMPCITY            EMPYEARS
            ------------------------------------
            Joe       Virginia Beach         2
            Jeff      Virginia Beach         1
            Wanda     Ocean City            10
            Fred      Ocean City             6
            Marvin    Wilmington             5
            Nick      Myrtle Beach           1
            Sam       Charleston             7
            Susan     Charleston             1
```

The SQL procedure can be used during an interactive SAS session or within batch programs. Global statements, such as TITLE and OPTIONS, can be used in any SAS procedure, including the SQL procedure. See Chapter 5, "SQL Procedure," for more information on SAS statements that can be used with the SQL procedure.

The sample data used in this book are stored in permanent SAS data files (that is, tables) in a SAS data library. The complete name of each permanent table has two levels, for example, SQL.EMPLOYEE. The first-level name is a *libref* (data library reference) and associates a SAS data library with a specific table; in this book, the libref SQL is used. The second-level name identifies the specific table in the data library, which in the previous example was EMPLOYEE.

The SQL procedure can refer to the second-level name or to both of these names. When a second-level name is used alone, it usually points to a temporary table. You can create the data library referred to by the SQL libref by running the SQLUGDAT member of the SAS Sample Library that is included on your product installation tape.

Comparing the SQL Procedure with the SAS DATA Step and Other SAS Procedures

The SQL procedure can perform some of the operations provided by the DATA step and the PRINT, SORT, and SUMMARY procedures. The following SELECT statement displays total service years for each sales representative's city in the Employee table:

```
proc sql;
select empcity, sum(empyears) as totyears
   from sql.employee
   where emptitle='salesrep'
   group by empcity
   order by totyears;
```

```
                                                              1
            EMPCITY          TOTYEARS
            --------------------------
            Myrtle Beach            1
            Virginia Beach          3
            Wilmington              5
            Charleston              7
            Ocean City             16
```

Here is a SAS program that produces the same result.

```
proc summary data=sql.employee;
   where emptitle='salesrep';
   class empcity;
   var empyears;
   output out=sumyears sum=totyears;
run;

proc sort data=sumyears;
   by totyears;
run;
```

```
proc print data=sumyears noobs;
   var empcity totyears;
   where _type_=1;
run;
```

```
                                                               1
                   EMPCITY        TOTYEARS
                Myrtle Beach          1
                Virginia Beach        3
                Wilmington            5
                Charleston            7
                Ocean City           16
```

This example shows that the SQL procedure can achieve the same results as base SAS software but often with fewer and shorter statements. The SELECT statement just shown performs summation, grouping, sorting, and row selection. SQL takes care of the procedural details of getting the result so you do not have to. It also executes the query without the RUN statement and automatically displays the query's results without the PRINT procedure. The chapters that follow show you how to take advantage of SQL's power while using the SAS System.

Using PROC SQL Views in SAS Procedures

A PROC SQL *view* is a stored SELECT statement that is executed at run time. Any SAS procedure can read a view as if the view were a SAS data file; for this reason, views are often thought of as virtual tables. Once executed, a view displays data derived from existing tables, other views, or SAS/ACCESS views. PROC SQL views do not actually contain data as tables do.

The Ocity view in the next example consists of an SQL SELECT statement that retrieves data for employees who live in Ocean City. When the Ocity view name is used as input to the PRINT procedure, the view's SELECT statement is executed to build a SAS data file that becomes the PRINT procedure's input.

```
proc sql;
create view ocity as
   select empname, empcity, emptitle, empyears
      from sql.employee
      where empcity='Ocean City';

proc print data=ocity;
   sum empyears;
run;
```

```
                                                              1
        OBS    EMPNAME    EMPCITY     EMPTITLE    EMPYEARS

         1      Herb      Ocean City  president      28
         2      Betty     Ocean City  manager         8
         3      Wanda     Ocean City  salesrep       10
         4      Fred      Ocean City  salesrep        6
                                                  ========
                                                      52
```

Notice that a view does not need to be in the same SAS data library as the table from which it retrieves data. In the previous example, the view name was referred to by its second-level name, indicating that it is stored in the temporary WORK data library. However, it accesses data from the permanent table EMPLOYEE in the SAS data library called SQL.

PROC SQL views can save time for SAS users who are interested, for example, in a superset of data from multiple SAS data sets. Joining the data sets through a view enables users to retrieve just the data they need and prevents them from continually coding statements to omit unwanted columns and rows. These views often save space since a view definition is often quite small compared with the data that it accesses. Views are also useful for retrieving frequently requested data.

Chapter Summary

This chapter has introduced the basic terms and concepts used in the Structured Query Language and in the SQL procedure. It has shown how you use the SQL procedure with the SAS System software and compared it with the SAS DATA step. Finally, it has shown how you can use views created with the SQL procedure in other SAS procedures as if the views were SAS data files.

The next chapter focuses on the SELECT and VALIDATE statements, including

□ how you can use them to retrieve data from tables and views

□ how you can validate the syntax of those data queries.

Part 2

Usage Guide for the SQL Procedure

Chapter 2   **Retrieving Data with the SELECT Statement**

Chapter 3   **Creating and Modifying Tables and Views**

Chapter 4   **Using the Advanced Features of the SQL Procedure**

Chapter **2** Retrieving Data with the SELECT Statement

Introduction   11

Querying a Single Table   12
Introducing the SELECT Statement   12
Specifying Columns with the SELECT Clause   13
Specifying a Column Alias (SELECT Clause)   14
Specifying Arithmetic Expressions (SELECT Clause)   15
Specifying a Table Name (FROM Clause)   16
Grouping the Results (GROUP BY Clause)   17
Sorting the Results (ORDER BY Clause)   17

Specifying Rows with the WHERE Clause   19
Logical Operators AND, OR, and NOT   21
LIKE Condition   21
IN Condition   22
BETWEEN Condition   22
IS NULL or IS MISSING Condition   23

Specifying Rows with a HAVING Expression   23

Querying Multiple Tables   24
Joining Two Tables   24
Using Table Aliases   26
How Joins Are Performed   26
Joining a Table with Itself   29
Joining More Than Two Tables   30

Using Subqueries   31
Subqueries with the NOT IN Condition   32
Correlated Subqueries   32
Subqueries with the EXISTS Condition   33
Multiple Levels of Subquery Nesting   34

When to Use Joins and Subqueries   35

Using the VALIDATE Statement   36

Chapter Summary   37

Introduction

This chapter shows you how to use the SELECT statement to retrieve
information from tables. It also shows you how to validate the correctness of
your SELECT statement using the VALIDATE statement. The examples progress
from the simple to the complex, illustrating how the clauses and components of
each statement work.

  You can use the SELECT statement to retrieve data described by PROC SQL
views and SAS/ACCESS views (that is, *view descriptors*) in the same way you
retrieve data from tables. In Version 6 of the SAS System, these views are

collectively called *SAS data views.* In Version 6, SAS data sets are implemented to include SAS data files and SAS data views. In this chapter, be aware that you can substitute the name of a SAS data view for a table name in any of the SELECT statement examples.

Chapter 3, "Creating and Modifying Tables and Views," shows how to create and use PROC SQL views. Chapter 4, "Using the Advanced Features of the SQL Procedure," describes how to use SAS/ACCESS views.

Querying a Single Table

Most of the examples in this book use the Employee, Product, Customer, and Invoice tables listed and described in Appendix 1, "Sample Tables." These permanently stored tables contain information about a sample beach-supplies wholesale company. The examples assume that the reader is familiar with the contents and layout of the tables. You may find it useful to refer to Appendix 1 while reading the examples. The SAS code to create these tables is in the member SQLUGDAT in the SAS Sample Library.

Introducing the SELECT Statement

In its simplest form, the SELECT statement retrieves and displays data from a table, PROC SQL view, or SAS/ACCESS view. A SELECT statement is also called a *query-expression* (or *query* for short) because it queries or retrieves information from the SAS System or an external database management system (DBMS).

With a SELECT statement, you can select data that meet certain conditions, group the data, or specify an order and format for the data's output. A SELECT statement begins with the keyword SELECT and ends with a semicolon, as shown here.

```
SELECT column <, column>...
    FROM table | view <, table | view>...
    <WHERE expression>
    <GROUP BY column <, column>... >
    <HAVING expression>
    <ORDER BY column <, column>... > ;
```

In this chapter, a SELECT *clause* refers to the SELECT list that begins with the keyword SELECT and ends before the keyword FROM. The SELECT clause can contain one or more column names, arithmetic expressions, summary functions, and other items, which are also called *object-items* in this book. These items are described in the following sections; the other clauses in the SELECT statement are then described.

Specifying Columns with the SELECT Clause

The SELECT clause specifies the columns (or variables) to be selected from a table or view. The columns are displayed in the result table in the same order as specified in the SELECT clause. You can perform calculations on the data in a table's columns and display the query's result.

The following PRINT procedure displays the Product table as output:

```
proc print data=sql.product noobs;
run;
```

```
                                                                      1
              PRODNAME    PRODCOST    PRODLIST

              flippers        $16         $20
              jet ski      $2,150      $2,675
              kayak          $190        $240
              raft             $5          $7
              snorkel         $12         $15
              surfboard      $615        $750
              windsurfer   $1,090      $1,325
```

To select specific columns from this table using the SQL procedure, list the column names in the desired order of appearance, separated by commas. To specify a permanent table in the FROM clause, precede the table name with a libref that associates the table with its SAS data library. (For more information on librefs, see "CREATE Statement" and "table-name" in Chapter 5, "SQL Procedure.") This next query selects and displays the list price and product name from the Product table, as follows:

```
proc sql;
select prodlist, prodname
   from sql.product;
```

```
                                                                      1
                 PRODLIST  PRODNAME
                 -------------------
                      $20  flippers
                   $2,675  jet ski
                     $240  kayak
                       $7  raft
                      $15  snorkel
                     $750  surfboard
                   $1,325  windsurfer
```

The SQL procedure executes a query without using the RUN statement. It also automatically displays the query's result in the OUTPUT window (or sends it to a list file) without using the PRINT procedure. Notice too that a line separates the column names from the rows.

To select all the columns from a table, an asterisk (*) can be used in place of the column names. The order of the columns displayed matches the order of the columns in the table, as shown here:

```
proc sql feedback;
select * from sql.product;
```

```
                                                              1
          PRODNAME   PRODCOST  PRODLIST
          ------------------------------
          flippers        $16       $20
          jet ski      $2,150    $2,675
          kayak          $190      $240
          raft             $5        $7
          snorkel         $12       $15
          surfboard      $615      $750
          windsurfer   $1,090    $1,325
```

The SQL procedure output does not include the OBS column unless specified to do so with the NUMBER option, as described in Chapter 5.

The FEEDBACK option in the previous PROC SQL statement writes the expanded or transformed form of SELECT * to the SAS log, as shown here:

```
SAS LOG

COMMAND ===>

NOTE: Statement transforms to:

      select PRODUCT.PRODNAME, PRODUCT.PRODCOST, PRODUCT.PRODLIST
        from SQL.PRODUCT;
```

The table and column names are listed for each column in the Product table. Using the FEEDBACK option does not affect the procedure's output; it just causes more information to be displayed in the SAS log.

Specifying a Column Alias (SELECT Clause)

A *column alias* is a temporary, alternate name for a column. Aliases are used in some queries to name or rename columns, or to make them easier to read. Column aliases are one word long and optional; if you want, each column in the SELECT clause can have an alias. The keyword AS is used with the column alias in the SELECT clause to distinguish the alias from other column names.

In the following query, the result of the summary function SUM(EMPYEARS) is given an alias (TOTYEARS) so that the table produced has a column name for this column:

```
proc sql;
select empcity, sum(empyears) as totyears
   from sql.employee
   where emptitle='sales representative'
   group by empcity
   order by totyears;
```

```
                                                                    1
              EMPCITY           TOTYEARS
              -------------------------
              Myrtle Beach             1
              Virginia Beach           3
              Wilmington               5
              Charleston               7
              Ocean City              16
```

Without the alias TOTYEARS, the results produced by SUM(EMPYEARS) would have no column heading. Notice also that TOTYEARS is used in the ORDER BY clause. A column alias can be used in place of the column name in the GROUP BY and ORDER BY clauses. A column alias cannot, however, be used in the WHERE clause because the expression in the WHERE clause is evaluated before the items in the SELECT clause. Column aliases can also be used to enhance the appearance of query results; see "column-modifier" in Chapter 5 for additional information on improving the appearance of result tables.

Specifying Arithmetic Expressions (SELECT Clause)

Arithmetic expressions in the SELECT clause perform computations on numeric table columns. See "sql-expression" in Chapter 5 for more detailed information on arithmetic operators. The following query displays the percentage profit margin for each product sold at full list price:

```
proc sql;
select prodname, prodlist, prodcost,
       (prodlist-prodcost)/prodlist
   from sql.product;
```

```
                                                                       1
      PRODNAME   PRODLIST  PRODCOST
      ------------------------------------------
      flippers       $20       $16        0.2
      jet ski     $2,675    $2,150   0.196262
      kayak         $240      $190   0.208333
      raft            $7        $5   0.285714
      snorkel        $15       $12        0.2
      surfboard     $750      $615       0.18
      windsurfer  $1,325    $1,090   0.177358
```

Note that the profit margin column has no heading and that the decimal points are not aligned. The default display format for numeric columns is BEST., as shown in this table. See "column-modifier" in Chapter 5 for ways to customize and enhance the appearance of your query results.

Specifying a Table Name (FROM Clause)

The FROM clause of the SELECT statement specifies the table from which you retrieve data.* A permanent table name in the FROM clause is preceded by a libref referring to the table's SAS data library. Linking a table name with a library is called *qualifying the table*. The SQL procedure in this book uses the libref SQL to qualify permanent table names. Tables that are stored temporarily in the SAS WORK data library do not need to be qualified with a libref. This convention is consistent with other SAS procedures.

The following query selects all the columns and rows from the Customer table and displays the result table:

```
proc sql;
title 'Customer Table';
select * from sql.customer;
```

---

* Because views retrieve data in the same way as tables do, you can substitute a PROC SQL or SAS/ACCESS view name here for any instance of a table name. If you want to specify more than one table or view in the FROM clause, see "Querying Multiple Tables" later in this chapter.

```
                  Customer Table                      1

     CUSTNAME    CUSTNUM  CUSTCITY
     ---------------------------------------
     Beach Land       16  Ocean City
     Coast Shop        3  Myrtle Beach
     Coast Shop        5  Myrtle Beach
     Coast Shop       12  Virginia Beach
     Coast Shop       14  Charleston
     Del Mar           3  Folly Beach
     Del Mar           8  Charleston
     Del Mar          11  Charleston
     New Waves         3  Ocean City
     New Waves         6  Virginia Beach
     Sea Sports        8  Charleston
     Sea Sports       20  Virginia Beach
     Surf Mart       101  Charleston
     Surf Mart       118  Surfside
     Surf Mart       127  Ocean Isle
     Surf Mart       133  Charleston
```

Grouping the Results (GROUP BY Clause)

The GROUP BY clause of the SELECT statement directs the SQL procedure to process a table in the specified groups. The groups are identified by the values in the specified columns. A GROUP BY clause is used only when a query includes a summary function. In this query, the results of the summary function are grouped by the city name: that is, the total number of EMPYEARS for each city is computed with the SUM function.

```
proc sql;
select empcity, sum(empyears) as totyears
   from sql.employee
   where emptitle='sales representative'
   group by empcity;
```

```
                                              1

        EMPCITY          TOTYEARS
        --------------------------
        Charleston              7
        Myrtle Beach            1
        Ocean City             16
        Virginia Beach          3
        Wilmington              5
```

When you use summary functions, the GROUP BY clause is usually specified in the query. Without a GROUP BY clause, one summary value is produced for the entire table.

Sorting the Results (ORDER BY Clause)

The ORDER BY clause of the SELECT statement directs the SQL procedure to sort the query result. One or more sorting columns can be chosen. Ascending (ASC) is the default sorting order, and it sorts from the lowest to the highest value. Descending (DESC) sorts in the opposite order. A sorting order can be specified for each column in the ORDER BY clause. Any column in a table or view can be a sorting column, even expression columns or columns that are not named in the SELECT clause.

The sorting order for all values (including missing values) is determined by the current sorting table in base SAS software and by your host system. The SAS System default table sorts character data in alphabetic order and numeric data in ascending order. However, you can specify other sorting (or collating) sequences using the SORTSEQ= option, as described in Chapter 5. See the description of the SORT procedure in the *SAS Procedures Guide, Version 6, Third Edition* and your host system documentation for information on other sorting sequences.

The following query displays the Product table sorted by ascending list price:

```
proc sql;
select prodname, prodlist, prodcost
    from sql.product
    order by prodlist;
```

```
                                                              1
        PRODNAME    PRODLIST  PRODCOST
        -------------------------------
        raft            $7        $5
        snorkel        $15       $12
        flippers       $20       $16
        kayak         $240      $190
        surfboard     $750      $615
        windsurfer  $1,325    $1,090
        jet ski     $2,675    $2,150
```

Do not confuse the sorting order of the rows with the display order of the columns in the result table. In the previous example, the order of the columns in the result table follows the order of the SELECT clause list. The values in the PRODLIST column follow the ascending sorting order specified in the ORDER BY clause. Because of the comparable values between the PRODLIST and PRODCOST columns in this example, the PRODCOST column also appears to sort in ascending order, although it has not been explicitly instructed to do so.

You can also specify multiple items in the ORDER BY clause. In the next example, the table is sorted first in descending order by the fourth item (percentage profit margin) in the SELECT clause list and then in ascending order by the PRODCOST column. (The number 4 is used in the ORDER BY clause because profit margin is an expression and therefore has no column name.) This query computes the percentage profit margin for each product sold at full list price:

```
select prodname, prodlist, prodcost,
        (prodlist-prodcost)/prodlist
    from sql.product
    order by 4 desc, prodcost asc;
```

```
                                                              1
     PRODNAME    PRODLIST  PRODCOST
     -------------------------------------------------
     raft             $7        $5   0.285714
     kayak          $240      $190   0.208333
     snorkel         $15       $12        0.2
     flippers        $20       $16        0.2
     jet ski      $2,675    $2,150   0.196262
     surfboard      $750      $615       0.18
     windsurfer   $1,325    $1,090   0.177358
```

Notice in this query that the PROC SQL statement is not repeated. You do not need to repeat the PROC SQL statement with each query unless you specify a DATA step or another SAS procedure between the queries.

The first column listed in the ORDER BY clause determines the primary row order of the result table. The second or later columns affect the order of the rows without overriding the primary order. In the previous example, the rows for `flippers` and `snorkel` have the same value in the fourth column. Because PRODCOST is sorted in ascending order, the row containing `snorkel` is output before the row containing `flippers` because the snorkel costs less than the flippers.

Another way to specify the result of (PRODLIST-PRODCOST)/PRODLIST is to give it a column alias, for example, PROFMARG. The alias becomes the column heading for the fourth column of the result table. You could then use either 4 or the alias to specify the column in the ORDER BY clause.

Specifying Rows with the WHERE Clause

While the SELECT clause specifies columns in a table, the WHERE clause specifies rows (or observations). The WHERE clause consists of the keyword WHERE and one or more *predicates*:

WHERE *predicate* <*operator predicate*> <<*operator predicate*>... >

Predicates are composed of different kinds of expressions and conditions. Therefore, a WHERE clause is also called a *WHERE expression*. When you specify more than one predicate, it is called a *compound predicate*.

When a row satisfies the expressions or conditions listed in the predicate (that is, it evaluates to true), the row is displayed in the result table. The following list shows various kinds of WHERE expressions:

`where a>b`	uses a comparison operator
`where a=10`	compares to a constant value
`where (a>b)&(c<d)`	uses comparison and logical operators in a compound predicate
`where (prodlist-prodcost)>100`	compares an arithmetic expression to a constant value
`where prodcost between 5 and 15`	tests for a range of values

```
where custcity not in              tests membership in a set of values
      ('Charleston','Surfside')

where invqty<(select max(invqty)   compares a variable to a value
             from sql.invoice      returned by a subquery
             where prodname=
                   'raft')

where empboss is null              tests for a missing value

where empname like 'c%'            tests for an item matching a pattern
```

A WHERE expression allows you to focus the results of your query so that you get only the information you need. For example, this query on the Employee table displays only those employees who have ten or more years of service.

```
proc sql;
select empname, emptitle
   from sql.employee
   where empyears>=10
   order by empname;
```

```
                                                              1
         EMPNAME   EMPTITLE
         --------------------
         Chuck     manager
         Herb      president
         Wanda     salesrep
```

Notice that in this example, the column specified in the WHERE expression is not specified in the SELECT clause. You can specify any column in the WHERE expression that exists in the named table or view.

In the previous WHERE clause, EMPYEARS>=10 is a predicate that contains a comparison operator. *Comparison operators* can be used in predicates that involve character and numeric columns. When complex arithmetic expressions are compared (that is, expressions using comparison operators), they can be grouped using parentheses. Grouping is recommended because it makes the expressions easier to read and avoids programming errors. Here are some of the comparison operators used in the SQL procedure:

=	equal to
¬= or ^=	not equal to
>	greater than
<	less than
>=	greater than or equal to
<=	less than or equal to

WHERE clause predicates that use comparison operators are called comparison predicates.

In addition to comparison operators, WHERE expressions can include other kinds of operators and conditions, as described in the following sections.

Logical Operators AND, OR, and NOT

To construct a compound predicate, connect single predicates in the WHERE expression using the logical operators AND, OR, or NOT. This query displays employees who neither live in Ocean City nor function as sales representatives but who have more than ten service years.

```
proc sql;
select empname, emptitle, empcity, empyears
   from sql.employee
   where (not (empcity='Ocean City' or emptitle='salesrep'))
         and (empyears>10);
```

```
                                                               1
     EMPNAME   EMPTITLE   EMPCITY        EMPYEARS
     --------------------------------------------------
     Chuck     manager    Charleston          12
```

Notice that when a constant character value, such as `Ocean City`, is used in a query, it is always enclosed in single or double quotes. This practice is consistent with other SAS System usage.

LIKE Condition

Using the LIKE condition in a WHERE expression, you can select table rows by comparing character-string columns to a pattern-matching specification. The LIKE condition is case-sensitive: that is, when it searches for a pattern to match, it distinguishes between uppercase and lowercase characters. This query displays each employee whose name begins with the uppercase letter S.

```
proc sql;
select empname
   from sql.employee
   where empname like 'S%';
```

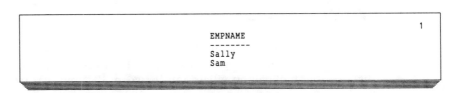

```
                                                               1
                      EMPNAME
                      --------
                      Sally
                      Sam
```

The percent sign (%) in this pattern specification matches any number of characters.

An underscore (_) in the specification matches just one arbitrary character. For example, this query selects each employee whose name ends with a lowercase k and consists of exactly four letters.

```
select empname
   from sql.employee
   where empname like '___k';
```

```
                                                                    1
                           EMPNAME
                           --------
                           Nick
```

IN Condition

The IN condition selects rows in which the column value is found in a set of values. This query displays employees who have worked for one, five, or ten years.

```
proc sql;
select empname, empyears
   from sql.employee
   where empyears in (1,5,10);
```

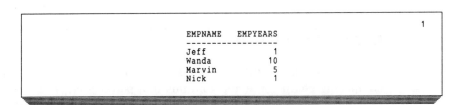

```
                                                                    1
                        EMPNAME    EMPYEARS
                        ------------------
                        Jeff              1
                        Wanda            10
                        Marvin            5
                        Nick              1
```

The IN condition is used to include a subquery that returns multiple values. See "Using Subqueries" later in this chapter and "sql-expression" in Chapter 5 for examples and more information. The IN condition can also be used in the SELECT and HAVING clauses. See "in-condition" in Chapter 5 for more information.

BETWEEN Condition

The BETWEEN condition selects rows in which column values are within a range of values. In this query, the BETWEEN range selects and displays all the rows whose employee numbers fall between 301 and 401, inclusively.

```
proc sql;
select empnum, empname
   from sql.employee
   where empnum between 301 and 401;
```

```
                                                                    1
                         EMPNUM   EMPNAME
                         ------------------
                            301   Sally
                            314   Marvin
                            318   Nick
                            401   Chuck
```

IS NULL or IS MISSING Condition

The IS NULL condition selects rows in which a column value is missing or null. For compatibility with the SAS System, you can specify the condition as IS NULL or IS MISSING. (NULL is the term used by other SQL implementations and MISSING is the SAS term.) The following query displays employees who have no supervisor: that is, the EMPBOSS column has a missing value instead of a supervisor's employee number.

```
proc sql;
select empname, empboss
   from sql.employee
   where empboss is null;
```

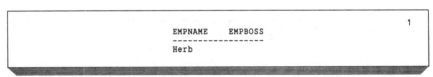

```
                                                                    1
                         EMPNAME    EMPBOSS
                         ------------------
                         Herb
```

In the SAS System, a period (.) indicates a missing numeric value and a blank space indicates a missing character value. Notice that IS MISSING qualifies all missing values (., .A, .B, and so on). The keywords NULL and MISSING both represent missing SAS values. For more information on missing values, see *SAS Language and Procedures: Usage, Version 6, First Edition*.

Specifying Rows with a HAVING Expression

A HAVING expression operates on entire groups of data, such as cities, rather than on single rows. You can think of a HAVING expression as a WHERE expression for groups. Only groups whose HAVING expression evaluates to true are displayed. A GROUP BY clause usually precedes a HAVING expression and defines the group that the HAVING expression evaluates. A HAVING expression can be used in either queries or subqueries.

A HAVING expression is used when a query includes a statistical summary function, such as COUNT in the next example. COUNT is the SQL name for the N and FREQ functions in the SAS System, which report (that is, count) the number of nonmissing arguments.

The following query lists customers and store numbers for customers with two stores each:

```
proc sql;
select custname, custnum, custcity
   from sql.customer
   group by custname
   having count(*)=2
   order by custname;
```

```
                                                                1
         CUSTNAME      CUSTNUM  CUSTCITY
         ------------------------------------
         New Waves          3  Ocean City
         New Waves          6  Virginia Beach
         Sea Sports        20  Virginia Beach
         Sea Sports         8  Charleston
```

In this query, the COUNT(*) function first counts all the stores that each customer has and then displays only those customers that have two stores (=2) in the result table. It then adds the cities in which the stores are located and their customer numbers as specified in the SELECT clause.

Querying Multiple Tables

You often need data that are stored in separate tables.* For example, you need to produce a report that links the sales figures in the Invoice table with the sales representatives' names in the Employee table. Information from separate tables can be combined by matching values in columns that relate the tables. This operation is called joining tables and is similar to, though not the same as, merging SAS data sets. *Joins* can be performed on up to 16 tables in one query.

You can also retrieve data from a table based on data values in another table by using nested queries called *subqueries*. The ability to nest queries is the basis for the word *structured* in Structured Query Language. Subqueries are described later in this chapter.

Joining Two Tables

The following query shows the cost, invoice price, and list price for each product sold to Beach Land stores. Part of the information, the cost and list price, is in the Product table; the other part, the invoice price, is in the Invoice table. The column that is common to both tables is PRODNAME. Therefore, to get all the information needed for the report, the tables must be joined together by matching rows that have common product names. The matching of these two

---

* For simplicity, table is used in this description to mean the following: table, PROC SQL view, or SAS/ACCESS view.

columns is performed by the PRODUCT.PRODNAME=INVOICE.PRODNAME condition in the WHERE expression.

```
proc sql;
select invnum, product.prodname, prodcost, invprice, prodlist,
       custname, custnum
    from sql.product, sql.invoice
    where product.prodname=invoice.prodname
          and custname='Beach Land';
```

```
                                                                  1
INVNUM  PRODNAME   PRODCOST  INVPRICE  PRODLIST  CUSTNAME    CUSTNUM
-------------------------------------------------------------------
   280  snorkel        $12       $14       $15   Beach Land       16
   290  flippers       $16       $19       $20   Beach Land       16
   300  raft            $5        $7        $7   Beach Land       16
```

Whenever two or more table names appear in the FROM clause, a join is being performed.

To avoid an ambiguous column reference, you must precede a column name that appears in more than one of the tables being joined with a table name. Connecting the table name to the column reference with a period is called *qualifying the column*. In the previous query, PRODUCT.PRODNAME means the following: the column PRODNAME from the table PRODUCT. Notice in the resulting table that PRODNAME is not qualified by its table name.

It is sometimes necessary to join tables by more than one column. For instance, joining the Customer and Invoice tables requires matching by both the customer name and the customer number because customer stores are uniquely identified by customer name-number combinations. This next query lists sales made to the Ocean City stores. It is necessary to refer to the Customer table because its CUSTCITY column is not duplicated in the Invoice table.

```
select invoice.custname, invoice.custnum, custcity,
       invnum, prodname
    from sql.invoice, sql.customer
    where invoice.custname=customer.custname and
          invoice.custnum=customer.custnum and
          custcity='Ocean City';
```

```
                                                        1
CUSTNAME    CUSTNUM  CUSTCITY      INVNUM  PRODNAME
---------------------------------------------------------
Beach Land       16  Ocean City       280  snorkel
Beach Land       16  Ocean City       290  flippers
Beach Land       16  Ocean City       300  raft
New Waves         3  Ocean City       450  flippers
New Waves         3  Ocean City       460  flippers
```

Using Table Aliases

A *table alias* is a temporary, alternate name for a table. You can specify table aliases in the FROM clause, often using the keyword AS to distinguish the table alias from other table names; however, this keyword is optional. Table aliases are used in joins to qualify column names so that the correct columns will be processed. Column names must be qualified using a table name or table alias when tables are joined that have at least one matching column name in the SELECT clause.

Table aliases are also used to reduce the number of keystrokes in a query. The previous example could be rewritten with tables aliases, as follows:

```
proc sql;
select i.custname, i.custnum, custcity,
       invnum, prodname
   from sql.invoice as i, sql.customer as c
   where i.custname=c.custname and
         i.custnum=c.custnum and
         custcity='Ocean City';
```

How Joins Are Performed

A query with a join and a WHERE expression is evaluated in two phases. First, the FROM clause is processed. SQL internally builds a virtual, temporary join table by combining each row from the first table with every row from the second table. The result of this combination is the *Cartesian product* of the two tables. Next, the WHERE expression is processed. Rows that satisfy the WHERE clause predicate are selected from this join table.

While it is helpful to imagine that SQL builds a temporary, internal join table for every join, this is often not the case. Depending on the tables and the SQL query, more efficient methods are often used. For more details, see "Improving Query Performance" in Chapter 4.

To avoid undesirable results, take care when constructing join queries. In each of the previous join queries, there is one table that has unique values in the join columns; for example, there are no duplicate customer name-number combinations within the Customer table. When at least one table has nonduplicate matching values, then the join is similar to a SAS data set merge or a table lookup.

The following examples show what happens when you join tables that have duplicate values in matching columns. The two tables used in the examples are created and displayed, with the Pet table being created first. See "CREATE Statement" and "INSERT Statement" in Chapter 5 for more information on these statements.

The Pet table is created and displayed, as follows:

```
proc sql;
create table sql.pet
   (person char,
    pettype char (12));

insert into sql.pet
   values('Jack','collie')
   values('Jack','parakeet')
   values('Sue','horse')
   values('Sue','goldfish');

title 'Pet Table';
select * from sql.pet;
```

```
                        Pet Table                        1

            PERSON    PETTYPE
            ---------------------
            Jack      collie
            Jack      parakeet
            Sue       horse
            Sue       goldfish
```

The City table is then created and displayed:

```
create table sql.city
   (person char,
    cityname char (12));

insert into sql.city
   values('Jack','Atlanta')
   values('Jack','Washington')
   values('Sue','Cary')
   values('Sue','Raleigh');

title 'City Table';
select * from sql.city;
```

```
                        City Table                       1

            PERSON    CITYNAME
            ---------------------
            Jack      Atlanta
            Jack      Washington
            Sue       Cary
            Sue       Raleigh
```

This query joins the Pet and City tables by matching the PERSON column:

```
title 'Tables Joined with PROC SQL';
select pet.person,  pettype,
       city.person, cityname
   from sql.pet, sql.city
   where pet.person=city.person
   order by 1,2,3,4;
```

The FROM clause internally constructs the following join table. There are 16 rows in this internal table because each of the 4 rows in the Pet table are matched with each of the 4 rows in the City table.

```
PERSON   PETTYPE    PERSON   CITYNAME
-----------------------------------------

Jack     collie     Jack     Atlanta
Jack     collie     Jack     Washington
Jack     collie     Sue      Cary
Jack     collie     Sue      Raleigh
Jack     parakeet   Jack     Atlanta
Jack     parakeet   Jack     Washington
Jack     parakeet   Sue      Cary
Jack     parakeet   Sue      Raleigh
Sue      goldfish   Jack     Atlanta
Sue      goldfish   Jack     Washington
Sue      goldfish   Sue      Cary
Sue      goldfish   Sue      Raleigh
Sue      horse      Jack     Atlanta
Sue      horse      Jack     Washington
Sue      horse      Sue      Cary
Sue      horse      Sue      Raleigh
```

Notice the way the ORDER BY clause works here. When you specify an ORDER BY clause in the first column in the SELECT list, PET.PERSON, `Jack` precedes `Sue` in alphabetic order. The second ordering column, PETTYPE, causes `collie` to come before `parakeet` for `Jack`, and `goldfish` to precede `horse` for `Sue`; at first glance, one may expect the opposite order because the row with `horse` precedes `goldfish` in the Pet table. The third ordering column, CITY.PERSON, again lists `Jack` before `Sue`. The fourth ordering column, CITYNAME, lists the cities alphabetically by the respective city names, `Atlanta` before `Washington` and `Cary` before `Raleigh`.

Next, the WHERE expression selects eight rows in which PET.PERSON is equal to CITY.PERSON. The result has multiple rows for each person because the Pet and City tables both have duplicate values in the PERSON column. Compare the results of the SQL table join with that of the SAS DATA step (following it) to see the difference between the two results.

The SQL table join produces this table.

```
                    Tables Joined with PROC SQL                     1

        PERSON    PETTYPE      PERSON    CITYNAME
        -----------------------------------------------
        Jack      collie       Jack      Atlanta
        Jack      collie       Jack      Washington
        Jack      parakeet     Jack      Atlanta
        Jack      parakeet     Jack      Washington
        Sue       goldfish     Sue       Cary
        Sue       goldfish     Sue       Raleigh
        Sue       horse        Sue       Cary
        Sue       horse        Sue       Raleigh
```

In a SAS DATA step (assuming that each SAS data set has been sorted BY PERSON), the later instance of `Jack` or `Sue` overwrites the previous instance. This SAS program produces the next table.

```
data;
   merge sql.pet sql.city;
   by person;
run;


proc print;
   title 'Tables Merged with the DATA Step';
run;
```

```
                Tables Merged with the DATA Step                    1

        OBS    PERSON    PETTYPE    CITYNAME

         1     Jack      collie     Atlanta
         2     Jack      parakeet   Washington
         3     Sue       horse      Cary
         4     Sue       goldfish   Raleigh
```

Here, the SAS MERGE statement acts differently than the SQL procedure. MERGE matches values (BY PERSON) and checks for duplicate values. When it finds a matching value, it performs a one-to-one merge on both the SAS data sets and outputs an observation. The PROC SQL result table, on the other hand, demonstrates the Cartesian product with its duplicate PERSON values and every possible combination of the result rows.

Joining a Table with Itself

Joining a table with itself allows you to look at a single table and manipulate it to get more information. You can think of the join of a table with itself as involving the production and then joining of two copies of the table. Table aliases are always required so that SQL can distinguish which copy of a table is being referenced. This kind of join is also called a *reflexive join*.

Joining a table with itself allows you to get different kinds of information from the same table. For example, in the Employee table, it is not immediately apparent which employee reports to which supervisor. By joining the table with itself, you can get this information in a glance. This following query displays the supervisor name for each employee who has a supervisor. The Employee table is joined with itself by matching the EMPBOSS column for each subordinate employee to the EMPNUM column of his or her supervisor. The subordinate employees are in the EMP copy of the table and the supervisors are in the MGR copy of the table.

```
select emp.empnum, emp.empname, emp.emptitle,
       mgr.empnum as mgrnum, mgr.empname as mgrname,
       mgr.emptitle as mgrtitle
   from sql.employee emp, sql.employee mgr
   where emp.empboss=mgr.empnum
   order by 1;
```

```
                                                               1
EMPNUM  EMPNAME  EMPTITLE    MGRNUM  MGRNAME   MGRTITLE
---------------------------------------------------------------
   201  Betty    manager        101  Herb      president
   213  Joe      salesrep       201  Betty     manager
   214  Jeff     salesrep       201  Betty     manager
   215  Wanda    salesrep       201  Betty     manager
   216  Fred     salesrep       201  Betty     manager
   301  Sally    manager        101  Herb      president
   314  Marvin   salesrep       301  Sally     manager
   318  Nick     salesrep       301  Sally     manager
   401  Chuck    manager        101  Herb      president
   417  Sam      salesrep       401  Chuck     manager
```

Notice that **Herb**, the president, does not appear in the EMPNAME column because he has no manager. See "Outer Joins" in Chapter 4 for information on including nonmatching values in joined tables.

Joining More Than Two Tables

The Employee and Customer tables are logically related to the Invoice table by the columns EMPNUM, CUSTNAME, and CUSTNUM. These common columns can be used to compose a query that retrieves information from all three tables. This query lists sales made by **Sam** to customer stores located in **Charleston**.

```
proc sql;
select c.custname, c.custnum, i.prodname,
       i.invnum, e.empname, c.custcity
   from sql.invoice i, sql.employee e, sql.customer c
   where i.empnum=e.empnum and i.custname=c.custname
         and i.custnum=c.custnum and e.empname='Sam'
         and c.custcity='Charleston'
   order by 1,2,3;
```

```
                                                                  1
CUSTNAME    CUSTNUM  PRODNAME    INVNUM  EMPNAME  CUSTCITY
----------------------------------------------------------------
Coast Shop       14  windsurfer     380  Sam      Charleston
Del Mar           8  raft           410  Sam      Charleston
Del Mar          11  flippers       440  Sam      Charleston
Del Mar          11  raft           420  Sam      Charleston
Del Mar          11  snorkel        430  Sam      Charleston
Surf Mart       101  snorkel        500  Sam      Charleston
Surf Mart       101  snorkel        520  Sam      Charleston
Surf Mart       101  surfboard      510  Sam      Charleston
```

The Customer table is joined to the Invoice table over the CUSTNAME and CUSTNUM columns, that is, the first two columns in the SELECT clause. This two-way internal join table is then joined with the Employee table over the EMPNUM column. The result is a three-way join table built from the Employee, Customer, and Invoice tables. From this join, rows are selected in which EMPNAME is `Sam` and CUSTCITY is `Charleston`.

Using Subqueries

While a table join combines multiple tables into a new table, a subquery (enclosed in parentheses) selects rows from one table based on values in another table. A *subquery*, or inner query, is a query-expression that is nested as part of another query-expression. Depending on the clause that contains it, a subquery can return a single value or multiple values. Subqueries are most often used in the WHERE and the HAVING expressions. See "sql-expression" in Chapter 5 for additional information on subqueries.

The following query uses a subquery to connect the names `Fred` and `Marvin` in the Employee table with their employee numbers in the Invoice table; the employee numbers appear in both tables and therefore link the tables. The subquery is evaluated first and selects Fred's and Marvin's employee numbers from the Employee table; these numbers are then used in the WHERE expression of the outer query to select rows from the Invoice table.

```
proc sql;
select empnum, custname, custnum,
       prodname, invnum
   from sql.invoice
   where empnum in
         (select empnum
             from sql.employee
             where empname in ('Fred','Marvin'))
   order by 1,2,3,4;
```

In this example, the subquery first builds a virtual, internal table consisting of Fred's and Marvin's employee numbers, which are 216 and 314. These two values become the set of values for the IN condition in the WHERE expression, as if the query had been written as follows:

```
select empnum, custname, custnum, prodname, invnum
   from sql.invoice
   where empnum in (216,314)
   order by 1,2,3,4;
```

The query is evaluated and displays the sales made by Fred and Marvin.

```
                                                               1
        EMPNUM  CUSTNAME   CUSTNUM  PRODNAME    INVNUM
        ---------------------------------------------
           216  Beach Land      16  flippers       290
           216  Beach Land      16  raft           300
           314  Surf Mart      127  flippers       560
           314  Surf Mart      127  surfboard      570
```

Subqueries with the NOT IN Condition

You have seen an example using the IN condition in WHERE expressions. You can also use the NOT IN condition to test if the values returned by the subquery satisfy the predicate. This example lists products that did not sell.

```
select prodname
    from sql.product
    where prodname not in
          (select prodname from sql.invoice)
    order by 1;
```

```
                                                               1
                         PRODNAME
                         ----------
                         jet ski
```

The subquery returns all the products in the Invoice table. This set of values is then compared with the list of products in the Product table. The values that appear in the Product table but not in the Invoice table are displayed in the resulting table.

Correlated Subqueries

When values returned by a subquery depend on values in the current row of an outer query, you have a *correlated subquery*: that is, rows in the subquery refer to and depend on values returned in the outer query. For example, this query displays employee information about sales representatives who sold surfboards.

```
proc sql;
select empnum, empname, empcity
    from sql.employee as e
    where 'surfboard' in
          (select prodname
               from sql.invoice as i
               where i.empnum=e.empnum)
    order by 1;
```

```
                                                                      1
        EMPNUM  EMPNAME  EMPCITY
        ------------------------------------
           213  Joe      Virginia Beach
           314  Marvin   Wilmington
           417  Sam      Charleston
```

A correlated subquery is evaluated for each row of the outer query because it refers to the values of columns in the outer query. For example, take the third row of the Employee table, which is referenced in the outer query. The third row in this table is for `Joe`, whose employee number is 213. E.EMPNUM in the subquery is replaced by 213 from the outer query. Therefore, for the third row, the subquery becomes the following:

```
(select prodname
     from sql.invoice as i
     where i.empnum=213)
```

This subquery is executed, building an internal table containing all products sold by employee 213 (`Joe`): rafts, snorkels, and surfboards. When **surfboard** (the constant in the WHERE clause of the outer query) is in this list of products for employee 213, the WHERE expression for the outer query evaluates to true, and the third row is displayed. The subquery is repeatedly evaluated, as described, for each row of the outer query, resulting in the display of only those rows in which PRODNAME is **surfboard**.

Subqueries with the EXISTS Condition

The EXISTS condition tests for the existence of a set of values described by the subquery. An EXISTS condition is true if any rows are produced in the evaluation of the subquery and false if no rows are produced. Conversely, the NOT EXISTS condition is true when a subquery evaluates to an empty table. This query lists the stores that did not buy their products from our sample wholesale company.

```
proc sql;
select distinct custname, custnum
   from sql.customer c
   where not exists
          (select *
               from sql.invoice i
               where i.custname=c.custname and
                     i.custnum=c.custnum)
   order by 1,2;
```

```
                                                                        1
      CUSTNAME     CUSTNUM
      --------------------
      Sea Sports          8
      Sea Sports         20
      Surf Mart         133
```

The previous example uses the keyword DISTINCT to remove duplicate items from the result table. Without it, the result table would include every occurrence of the customer name and number returned by the query.

Also notice the use of the correlated references to C.CUSTNAME and C.CUSTNUM in this subquery. Because the subquery is evaluated for each row in the outer table, the subquery may produce an output row for one customer and no row for another customer.

The following steps are taken to process each row of the outer query. Take, for example, the eleventh row of the Customer table. The subquery matches the customer name and number values, **Sea Sports** and 8, from the eleventh row of the Customer table with the values in the Invoice table. For this row of the outer query, the subquery becomes the following:

```
(select *
    from sql.invoice i
    where i.custname='Sea Sports' and
          i.custnum=8)
```

Since the subquery evaluates to an empty table, the NOT EXISTS condition is true and the eleventh row of the Customer table is selected for the result table. The outer query and then subquery are repeatedly evaluated, as described, until the Customer table ends and no more rows can be selected.

Multiple Levels of Subquery Nesting

Subqueries can be nested so that the innermost subquery returns value(s) to be used by the next outer query. Then, that subquery's value(s) will be used by the next outer query, and so on. Evaluation always begins with the innermost subquery and works outward.

This query displays the employee numbers and names of sales representatives who made sales to stores in Ocean City.

```
proc sql;
select empnum, empname                                    ┐
   from sql.employee                                      │  outer query
   where empnum in                                        ┘
           (select empnum                                 ┐
               from sql.invoice i                         │  middle query
               where 'Ocean City' in ──────────           ┘
                   (select custcity                       ┐
                       from sql.customer c                │
                       where c.custname=i.custname  and   │  inner query
                       c.custnum=i.custnum))              ┘
       order by 1;                                          outer query
```

```
                                                                  1
            EMPNUM  EMPNAME
            ------------------
               215  Wanda
               216  Fred
```

In this example, the innermost subquery is evaluated for each row in the Invoice table and returns the customer city for that invoice. The middle-level subquery returns the employee numbers for all sales representatives who sold to Ocean City stores. The outer query displays employee rows in which the employee number is in the list of numbers found by the middle-level query.

When to Use Joins and Subqueries

Use a join or a subquery any time you reference information from multiple tables. Joins and subqueries are often used together in the same query. In many cases, you can solve a data retrieval problem by using a join, a subquery, or both.

Some guidelines for when to use joins and queries are given here.

□ If you need data for your report that is from more than one table, you have to perform a join. Whenever multiple tables (or views) are listed in the FROM clause, those tables become joined.

□ If you need to combine related information from different rows within a table, you can join the table with itself to get it. See "Joining a Table with Itself" earlier in this chapter.

□ Subqueries are used when the desired result would require more than one query and each subquery provides a subset of the table involved in the query.

□ If a membership type of question is asked, a subquery is usually used. An example of this sort is in "Subqueries with the EXISTS Condition" earlier in this chapter. If the query requires a NOT EXISTS condition, you must use a subquery because NOT EXISTS operates only in a subquery; the same principle holds true for the EXISTS condition.

□ Many queries can be formulated as joins or subqueries. Although the PROC SQL query optimizer changes some subqueries to joins, a join is generally more efficient to process.

Using the VALIDATE Statement

You can use the VALIDATE statement to check the correctness of your SELECT statement's syntax without actually executing the query. When you submit a query, it is written to the SAS log with a message indicating whether the query is valid or has produced a syntax error. If the SELECT statement produces an error or warning, the macro variable SQLRC (SQL return code) is set accordingly; this macro variable can be retrieved, if desired, as described later in this section. This example shows a query and the message produced in the SAS log.

```
proc sql;
validate
    select empnum, empname
        from sql.employee
        where empnum>200 and empnum<400;

NOTE: The PROC SQL syntax is valid.
```

If you leave a column name out of the last line of the query, as shown here, an error message is written to the SAS log. This example was run under the MVS/XA™ host system on an IBM computer; your results may differ depending on your host system.

MVS/XA is a trademark of International Business Machines Corporation.

```
SAS LOG

COMMAND ===>

16  proc sql;
17  validate
18    select empnum, empname
19      from sql.employee
20      where empnum > 200 and < 400;
                              -
                              1

ERROR: Expecting one of the following: NAME, "STRING", 1, 1.0,
       "01JAN60"D, "12:00"T, "01JAN60:12:00"DT, '.', USER.
       The statement is being ignored.
```

The VALIDATE statement can also be included in programs that use the macro facility. In this case, VALIDATE returns a value indicating a SELECT statement's validity. If your SELECT statement would be valid if executed, the SQL procedure sets the value of the macro variable SQLRC to 4 (a warning) or less.

Since the query on the previous page is valid, the SAS System would return a macro variable value of 0 for no errors. If the WHERE clause contained a reference to a column that did not exist in the Employee table, the SQLRC macro would return an 8 (for error) and the statement could not be executed. See Chapter 4 for more information on the macro facility interface and "host-variable" in Chapter 5 for more information on macro variables.

The VALIDATE statement is useful for building applications where you can enter all or part of a PROC SQL statement. The application can then preprocess the user requests (or queries) to determine whether the request is valid.

Chapter Summary

This chapter has introduced the SELECT and VALIDATE statements as well as some of their clauses and components. It has covered the following topics:

□ the SELECT clause, specifying columns, column aliases, and arithmetic expressions; the FROM clause with single and multiple tables; and the GROUP BY and ORDER BY clauses

□ the WHERE expression with logical and comparison operators and the following predicates: BETWEEN condition, IN condition, IS NULL condition, and LIKE condition

□ the HAVING clause, whose expressions are evaluated once for each group listed in the query

□ joins and how they work, joins on two and three tables, and joining a table with itself

□ subqueries and how they work, including correlated subqueries, those with multiple levels of nesting, and subqueries that use the EXISTS condition

□ the VALIDATE statement and its use with macro variables.

The next chapter describes how to use the ALTER, CREATE, DELETE, DESCRIBE, DROP, INSERT, RESET, and UPDATE statements to modify and create tables and views.

Chapter **3** Creating and Modifying Tables and Views

Introduction *39*

Creating a Table *40*
Deleting a Table   *42*

Creating and Using a View Definition *42*
Describing a View Definition   *44*
Deleting a View Definition   *45*
Coding a View In-Line   *45*
Using Views within Other SAS Procedures   *46*
Advantages of Using Views in SAS Programs   *48*

Creating and Using an Index *49*
Deleting an Index   *50*

Modifying a Table and Its Data *50*
Altering Columns in a Table   *50*
Updating Columns in a Table   *53*
Inserting Rows into a Table   *55*
Deleting Rows from a Table   *57*

Resetting SQL Procedure Options *57*

Chapter Summary *58*

Introduction

While Chapter 2, "Retrieving Data with the SELECT Statement," shows you how to perform and validate queries with the SELECT statement, this chapter shows you how to create and modify tables and views with the other statements of the SQL procedure.* It describes how to do the following:

- [] create tables, PROC SQL views, and indexes on table columns using the CREATE statement or drop them using the DROP statement

- [] display a view's definition using the DESCRIBE statement

- [] add new columns to a table or change the attributes of an existing column using the ALTER statement

- [] add or change the values in a table using the UPDATE statement

- [] add rows to a table using the INSERT statement or remove rows using the DELETE statement

- [] add, change, or remove any PROC SQL statement option using the RESET statement.

---

*   In this chapter, a view refers to a PROC SQL view; SAS/ACCESS views (or view descriptors) are distinguished from PROC SQL views.

This chapter also shows how certain SAS System features, such as dates, labels, and formats, are handled in the SQL procedure. In this chapter, the examples progress from the simple to complex, illustrating how the clauses and components of each statement work.

See Chapter 5, "SQL Procedure," for detailed descriptions of the SQL procedure options, statements, and components referred to in this chapter.

Creating a Table

You can use the CREATE statement to create tables, views, and indexes on table columns. This section focuses on the ways you can create SQL tables as temporary and permanent SAS data files.

The following example creates a table by using a query-expression in the CREATE TABLE statement.* When a table is created in this way, its data are derived from the table(s), view(s), or SAS/ACCESS view(s) referenced in the query-expression's FROM clause. The new table's column names are as specified in the query-expression's SELECT clause list. The column attributes (that is, type, length, informat, and format) are the same as those of the selected source columns.

Because the libref WORK is specified in this example's CREATE TABLE statement, the table is stored temporarily and will be erased when the SAS batch job or interactive session ends; since WORK is the default temporary libref, you can omit it from the statement. The Senior table contains employees who have worked for the sample wholesale company for more than six years and who are sales representatives.

```
proc sql;
create table work.senior as
    select empname, empyears, emptitle
        from sql.employee
        where empyears>=6 and
                emptitle='salesrep'
        order by empyears desc;

title 'Senior Sales Staff';
select * from work.senior;

NOTE:  Table WORK.SENIOR created, with 3 rows and 3 columns.
```

The note is written to the SAS log to let you know that your CREATE statement has executed successfully. The newly created table is not displayed in SAS output unless you perform a query (that is, a SELECT statement) on it. The SELECT * query displays the entire Senior table, as shown here.

---

* A query-expression is a SELECT statement with or without set operators. See "query-expression" in Chapter 5 for more information.

```
                      Senior Sales Staff                        1

              EMPNAME    EMPYEARS  EMPTITLE
              -----------------------------
              Wanda           10  salesrep
              Sam              7  salesrep
              Fred             6  salesrep
```

If this table were created permanently, you could refer to it in other queries and statements during other SAS jobs or sessions.

You can also create a table based on a single table, view, or SAS/ACCESS view using a LIKE clause with the CREATE TABLE statement. The new table's column names and column attributes are the same as those of its source. When a CREATE TABLE statement with the LIKE clause is executed, the new table is created with the same columns as described, but without rows. You can then use the INSERT statement to add rows to the new table or the ALTER statement to add columns or change the attributes of existing columns.

In the next example, the Subinv table duplicates the Invoice table. The SAS data set option DROP= causes the columns INVNUM and EMPNUM to be omitted from the new table; see "SQL Procedure and SAS Data Set Options" in Chapter 5 for more information. Notes are written to the SAS log.

```
create table sql.subinv(drop=invnum empnum)
   like sql.invoice;

select * from sql.subinv;

NOTE:  Table SQL.SUBINV created, with 0 rows and 5 columns.
NOTE:  No observations were selected.
```

As documented by the first note in the log, the Subinv table is created without rows of data. To duplicate another table and retain its data, use the form shown in the previous CREATE TABLE example titled Senior Sales Staff.

In the LIKE clause example, the Subinv table was created as a *permanent* SAS data file. To make a table a permanent SAS data file, you must precede the table name with a *libref* that points to a SAS data library; the libref must already have been assigned to the library before you can refer to it in a statement or query. In these examples, the table name SUBINV was preceded by the SAS data library name SQL. The four sample tables included with this book—EMPLOYEE, PRODUCT, CUSTOMER, and INVOICE—are also permanent SAS data files in a SAS data library referenced as SQL.

This next example uses a column-definition list (in parentheses) to define the columns and their attributes in the Rivals table. The column attributes defined are data type, length, informat, and format. The note is written to the SAS log.

```
proc sql;
create table sql.rivals
   (competit char(12),        /* competitor's name */
    compcity char(12),        /* competitor's city */
    custname char(12),        /* customer's name   */
    prodname char(12),        /* product name      */
    sale_mon num informat=dollar10.2
             format=dollar.); /* competitor's monthly sales */

NOTE:  Table SQL.RIVALS created, with 0 rows and 5 columns.
```

When the numbers in the SALE_MON column are displayed in SAS output, the DOLLAR. format specifies that seven numbers (the default) are allowed, including the dollar sign ($) and the comma; the numbers after the decimal point will not be displayed.

The format DOLLAR. is used to define how values in the table are displayed *every time* the table is referred to in a query. If you prefer more flexibility, you can omit the FORMAT= specification at the table's creation and specify it when the columns are listed in a query, as shown in the next example. The note is written to the SAS log.

```
select competit, compcity, custname, prodname,
        sale_mon format=dollar.
    from sql.rivals;

NOTE:  No observations were selected.
```

No result table is displayed because the Rivals table contains no data.

Deleting a Table

Tables are deleted using the DROP TABLE statement. This example deletes the Rivals table.

```
proc sql;
drop table sql.rivals;

NOTE: Table SQL.RIVALS has been dropped.
```

If Rivals had been a temporary table, you would need only to specify the table name itself, without the WORK libref. If you drop a table, particularly a permanent one, be sure to remove references to it in your other queries, views, and statements.

Creating and Using a View Definition

A PROC SQL view is a stored query-expression that is given a name. It is derived from one or more tables, views, or SAS/ACCESS views. When the PROC SQL view is referenced in a SELECT statement's FROM clause, the view is executed and a virtual, internal table is built by the SQL procedure. This internal table is then processed by the FROM clause.

For example, the following statements create and retrieve data using the temporarily stored view definition Bigsale; when the SAS interactive session or batch job ends, the view will be erased. The view's SELECT statement lists invoices in which the total sale amount exceeds $1500. The Employee table is joined with the Invoice table so that the employee name, instead of the employee number, can appear in the result table. The note is written to the SAS log.

```
proc sql;
create view bigsale as
    select invnum, custname, custnum, empname, prodname,
           invqty, invprice
       from sql.invoice as i, sql.employee as e
       where i.empnum=e.empnum and
             (invqty * invprice) > 1500;

select * from bigsale
    order by invnum;

NOTE:  View WORK.BIGSALE has been defined.
```

```
                                                        1
  INVNUM  CUSTNAME    CUSTNUM  EMPNAME  PRODNAME    INVQTY  INVPRICE
  --------------------------------------------------------------------
     310  Coast Shop        3  Nick     windsurfer      2    $1,305
     480  New Waves         6  Joe      surfboard       4      $735
     570  Surf Mart       127  Marvin   surfboard       3      $740
```

To the PROC SQL user, it appears that the PROC SQL view is a table because view names and table names can be used interchangeably in SELECT statements and other SAS procedures. For this reason, a view is often thought of as a virtual table. However, a view is not a table. A view is a stored query-expression while a table is stored data. Therefore, a view cannot be updated in the SQL procedure as you would update a table: that is, you cannot use the INSERT, DELETE, UPDATE, or ALTER statements when referencing a view. (Future releases of the SAS System will allow you to use a view to insert and delete rows and to update values in a view's underlying table(s); you will be able to make changes to source tables through a view.)

Views have a variety of uses. One use is to provide users with an alternate view of stored data. For instance, a group of users may only be concerned with data that pertain to their department. A view can be created that selects only the rows and columns of interest. The users retrieve data using the view name instead of the table name where the actual data is stored. This process may reduce the length of SQL queries and shield users from unwanted or confidential information.

Another use of views is to hide the details of large and complex joins. Also, an often-used join can be coded in a view once and referred to many times in succeeding queries to get the most current data available.

Permanently stored views can be created and referenced in the same way as permanently stored tables. To use a permanent view, precede the view name by a libref that points to a SAS data library; remember, the libref must already have been assigned to the library. The following statements create and display a permanent view named HIGHQTY, which is stored permanently in a SAS data library pointed to by the libref SQL:

```
proc sql;
create view sql.highqty as
   select *
       from sql.invoice
       where invqty>=25;


select * from sql.highqty;
```

```
                                                                 1
   INVNUM  CUSTNAME    CUSTNUM   EMPNUM   PRODNAME    INVQTY  INVPRICE
   -------------------------------------------------------------------
      320  Coast Shop       3      318   raft           30       $6
      350  Coast Shop       5      318   raft           40       $6
      390  Del Mar          3      417   flippers       30      $18
      410  Del Mar          8      417   raft           40       $6
      540  Surf Mart      118      318   raft           30       $6
      560  Surf Mart      127      314   flippers       25      $19
```

The libref on the Invoice table can be omitted in this example because the table and the view are both stored in the same SAS data library. See "Creating Views with the SQL Procedure" in Chapter 5 for more information on using librefs and storing views.

Describing a View Definition

The DESCRIBE statement displays the text of a query stored in a view definition. The following example prints the Highqty view definition in the SAS log:

```
proc sql;
describe view sql.highqty;
```

```
SAS LOG

COMMAND ===>

NOTE: View SQL.HIGHQTY is defined as:

      select *
          from SQL.INVOICE
          where INVQTY>=25;
```

Each view is described as you originally defined it. To see an expanded version of the Highqty view (that is, to list all the qualified columns in the SELECT clause) in the SAS log, use the FEEDBACK option on your PROC statement. This option is described and illustrated in "PROC SQL and RESET Statements" in Chapter 5.

Deleting a View Definition

View definitions are deleted using the DROP VIEW statement. This example creates and then deletes the Names view definition. Notes are written to the SAS log.

```
proc sql;
create view names as
    select prodname from sql.product;

NOTE: View WORK.NAMES has been defined.

drop view names;

NOTE: View WORK.NAMES has been dropped.
```

If you drop a view, particularly a permanent view, be sure to remove references to it in your other queries, view definitions, and statements.

Coding a View In-Line

In some cases, you may want to use a query-expression in a FROM clause instead of a simple table or view name. You can create a view as a query-expression and refer to it in your FROM clause, but that process involves two steps. An alternative way is to code the view in-line in the FROM clause, enclosing it in parentheses, and thereby saving the extra step.

An *in-line view* is a query-expression nested in a FROM clause. Unlike views created with the CREATE VIEW statement, in-line views are not assigned names and cannot be referenced in other queries or SAS procedures as if they were tables. An in-line view can be referenced only in the query in which it is defined.

Because this example includes an in-line view, a join, and a summary function, each step of its evaluation is described following the example. This query lists the sales representatives who have sold 20 or more rafts and the number of rafts that each sold.

```
proc sql;
select empname, numraft
    from (select empname, sum(invqty) as numraft
            from sql.invoice i, sql.employee e
            where prodname='raft' and
                    i.empnum=e.empnum
            group by empname)
    where numraft>=20
    order by 1;
```

As in subqueries, an in-line view is evaluated first. The view's SELECT statement creates a virtual, intermediate join table and uses the WHERE expression to evaluate each row of this table. Rows that include the PRODNAME **raft** and have employee numbers that match in the two tables are selected.

The SUM function in the SELECT clause list is then evaluated, adding the values in the INVQTY column for each group listed in the GROUP BY clause. For example, the values in the INVQTY column are added for the rows where `Nick` is the EMPNAME (with the matching EMPNUM 318) and the PRODNAME is `raft`. The internal table created by the in-line view is as follows:

```
EMPNAME    NUMRAFT
-------------------
Fred           20
Joe            10
Nick          100
Sam            55
```

The SELECT statement in the outer query then uses this internal table to evaluate its WHERE expression, select the columns, and order the rows. The row with EMPNAME `Joe` is omitted because it does not satisfy the WHERE expression. The final result table is then displayed.

```
                                                          1
        EMPNAME    NUMRAFT
        -------------------
        Fred           20
        Nick          100
        Sam            55
```

Using Views within Other SAS Procedures

Views can be used as input SAS data sets in all SAS procedures. This example uses the PRINT procedure to display the data defined by the Highqty view.

```
proc print data=sql.highqty noobs;
run;
```

```
                                                                         1
INVNUM    CUSTNAME    CUSTNUM    EMPNUM    PRODNAME    INVQTY    INVPRICE

  320     Coast Shop      3        318      raft         30         $6
  350     Coast Shop      5        318      raft         40         $6
  390     Del Mar         3        417      flippers     30        $18
  410     Del Mar         8        417      raft         40         $6
  540     Surf Mart     118        318      raft         30         $6
  560     Surf Mart     127        314      flippers     25        $19
```

While this statement is executing, the view passes rows one-by-one to the SAS PRINT procedure until the entire result table is displayed in SAS output.

The following example uses the CONTENTS procedure with the Highqty view. It and the next example are run under the MVS/XA host system on an IBM computer; the actual output will vary from system to system.

```
proc contents data=sql.highqty;
run;
```

```
                                                                        1
                            CONTENTS PROCEDURE
        Data Set Name: SQL.HIGHQTY            Observations:         .
        Member Type:   VIEW                   Variables:            7
        Engine:        SQLVIEW                Indexes:              0
        Created:       15DEC89:16:37:16       Observation Length:   72
        Last Modified: 15DEC89:16:37:16       Deleted Observations: 0
        Data Set Type:                        Compressed:           NO
        Label:

            -----Alphabetic List of Variables and Attributes-----

            #    Variable   Type   Len   Pos   Format
            ----------------------------------------------
            2    CUSTNAME   Char    10     8
            3    CUSTNUM    Num      8    24
            4    EMPNUM     Num      8    32
            1    INVNUM     Num      8     0
            7    INVPRICE   Num      8    64   DOLLAR.
            6    INVQTY     Num      8    56
            5    PRODNAME   Char    10    40
```

Notice that some fields in the top half of the CONTENTS procedure display have missing values, even though you know, for example, that this view contains observations (rows) when it is executed and its results are displayed in output. No observations are listed after Observations because this value refers to the actual data in the table; a view is a stored query-expression, not stored data.

When you compare the previous CONTENTS procedure output with that of the Highqty's underlying table (Invoice), you see the differences.

```
proc contents data=sql.invoice;
run;
```

```
                                                                          1
                           CONTENTS PROCEDURE
        Data Set Name: SQL.INVOICE          Observations:          30
        Member Type:   DATA                 Variables:             7
        Engine:        V606                 Indexes:               0
        Created:       14DEC89:16:39:35     Observation Length:    60
        Last Modified: 14DEC89:16:39:35     Deleted Observations:  0
        Data Set Type:                      Compressed:            NO
        Label:

               -----Alphabetic List of Variables and Attributes-----

                 #   Variable   Type   Len   Pos   Format
               ----------------------------------------------------
                 2   CUSTNAME   Char    10     8
                 3   CUSTNUM    Num      8    18
                 4   EMPNUM     Num      8    26
                 1   INVNUM     Num      8     0
                 7   INVPRICE   Num      8    52    DOLLAR.
                 6   INVQTY     Num      8    44
                 5   PRODNAME   Char    10    34


                   -----Engine/Host Dependent Information-----

        Data Set Page Size:         6144
        Number of Data Set Pages:   1
        First Data Page:            1
        Max Obs per Page:           84
        Obs in First Data Page:     30
        Physical Name:              SAS-DATA-LIBRARY
        Release created:            6.06
        Release last modified:      6.06
        Created:                    16:39 THURSDAY, DECEMBER 14, 1989
        Created by:                 SASUSER
        Last modified:              16:39 THURSDAY, DECEMBER 14, 1989
        Last modified by:           SASUSER
        Subextents:                 1
        Total blocks used:          1
```

Advantages of Using Views in SAS Programs

The use of views in SAS procedures can increase the power and flexibility of SAS programs:

□ Instead of using multiple DATA steps to merge SAS data sets by common variables, a view can be constructed that performs a multi-table join.

□ Disk space may be saved by storing a view definition, that is, only the definition itself and not the actual data.

□ Views can ensure that input data sets are always current because data from views are derived at execution time.

□ An Information Center can provide powerful views for use by the SAS user community, thereby avoiding the need for all users to learn SQL details.

□ Views can reduce the impact of data design changes on users. For example, you can change a query stored in a view without changing the characteristics of the view's result. If data stored in one table is separated into two tables for design improvements, a view on that single table can be changed so that it now joins the two tables. The view's result is the same, and the change has no impact on users who may reference the view in their programs.

□ With SAS/SHARE software, a view can join together SAS data sets that reside on different host computers, presenting the user with an integrated view of distributed company data.

Creating and Using an Index

An *index* stores the values of a table's columns and a system of directions that enable access to rows (in that table) by index value. Defining an index on a column or set of columns enables the SAS System, under certain circumstances, to access rows in a table more quickly and efficiently. In the SQL procedure, you create an index using the CREATE INDEX statement. Once you have created an index for one or more columns in a table, the SAS System determines when to use it in processing queries and statements. You cannot explicitly tell the SAS System to use an index in processing.

Once an index has been created for column(s) in a table, the SAS System treats it as part of the table. Therefore, if you insert or delete rows, the index is automatically updated.

You can create simple or composite indexes. A *simple index* is created on one column in a table and must have the same name as the column. It locates rows by the values of the one variable in the table. A simple index is typically defined on a column that lists an employee number, invoice number, or social security number in a table. This index can be on a column that holds numeric or character data. For example, the following statement creates an index on the INVNUM (invoice number) column of the Invoice table. The note is written to the SAS log.

```
proc sql;
create index invnum on sql.invoice(invnum);

NOTE:  Simple index INVNUM has been defined.
```

A *composite index* is created on two or more columns in a table. The columns can hold numeric or character data, or both, and they can appear in any order. (The order can affect whether the SAS System uses the composite index and how efficiently it performs. See "SAS Indexes" in Chapter 6, "SAS Files," of *SAS Language: Reference, Version 6, First Edition* for more information on these topics.) A composite index cannot have the same name as one of its columns. You can create more than one composite index on a table.

This composite index links the invoice number (INVNUM) with the number of the sales representative (EMPNUM) who made the sale. The note is written to the SAS log.

```
create index idnums on sql.invoice(invnum,empnum);

NOTE:  Composite index IDNUMS has been defined.
```

The UNIQUE keyword can be specified with either a simple or composite index definition. You use this optional keyword when the values in the row must be unique, for example, when processing a table that contains social security numbers. If a table contains multiple occurrences of the same value, the UNIQUE option will not be accepted and the index will not be defined on that column. If you have a uniquely defined index on a column and try to add a duplicate value to the table, the row will not be inserted.

This unique index is defined on the EMPNUM (employee number) column of the Employee table. The note is written to the SAS log.

```
create unique index empnum on sql.employee(empnum);

NOTE:  Simple index EMPNUM has been defined.
```

Deleting an Index

Indexes are deleted using the DROP INDEX statement. This example deletes the composite index IDNUMS (defined in the previous section) from the Invoice table. The note is written to the SAS log.

```
proc sql;
drop index idnums from sql.invoice;

NOTE: Index IDNUMS has been dropped.
```

See "Creating Indexes with the SQL Procedure" in Chapter 5 for more information on indexes. See also "SAS Indexes" in Chapter 6 of *SAS Language: Reference* for an extensive description of how to define and manage SAS indexes and how they affect other SAS statements.

Modifying a Table and Its Data

The SQL procedure gives you several statements with which to modify the structure of a table as well as the data within it. These statements apply only to tables (SAS data files) and not to PROC SQL views. In some cases, as noted, the statements can reference SAS/ACCESS views (that is, view descriptors). For more information on these SQL statements, see their individual descriptions in Chapter 5. For more information on SAS/ACCESS views, see "SAS/ACCESS Interface" in Chapter 4, "Using the Advanced Features of the SQL Procedure."

Altering Columns in a Table

The ALTER statement enables you to alter the attributes of columns in an existing table. It also enables you to add new columns to or drop columns from an existing table. Once you have defined new columns in a table, you can use the UPDATE statement to add values to them.

The following example creates and displays a permanent table so that it can be used to alter the display formats of the columns. The note is written to the SAS log.

```
proc sql;
create table sql.newprice as
    select prodname as product, prodcost as cost,
           prodlist label='List Price'
       from sql.product;

select * from sql.newprice;

NOTE: Table SQL.NEWPRICE has 7 rows and 3 columns.
```

Notice that when you use column aliases (PRODUCT and COST) in this form of the CREATE TABLE statement, the aliases actually rename the columns. When a label (List Price) is used for a column, the column name remains unchanged even though the label, not the column name, appears in output.

```
                                                               1
                                 List
            PRODUCT       COST    Price
            ------------------------------
            flippers       $16     $20
            jet ski    $2,150  $2,675
            kayak         $190    $240
            raft            $5      $7
            snorkel        $12     $15
            surfboard     $615    $750
            windsurfer $1,090  $1,325
```

You can now use the ALTER statement to add the column LIST1990. The column attributes for LIST1990 are defined along with the column: a numeric data type, 8 bytes in length, and the DOLLAR. format.

```
alter table sql.newprice
    add list1990 num format=dollar.;

select * from sql.newprice;
```

```
                                                               1
                                 List
            PRODUCT       COST    Price  LIST1990
            -----------------------------------------
            flippers       $16     $20          .
            jet ski    $2,150  $2,675          .
            kayak         $190    $240          .
            raft            $5      $7          .
            snorkel        $12     $15          .
            surfboard     $615    $750          .
            windsurfer $1,090  $1,325          .
```

You can then use the UPDATE statement, described later in "Updating Columns in a Table," to add values to the new column LIST1990.

You could create the Newprice table in another way, eliminating the UPDATE statement step, and use the ALTER statement to change the table's display format.* Take the previous example as a model and use an arithmetic expression to add the values in the LIST1990 column. This example adds 20% to the list price of all the 1990 products.

```
create table sql.newprice as
   select prodname as product, prodcost as cost,
          prodlist label='List Price',
          (prodlist*1.2) as list1990 format=dollar.
      from sql.product;

select * from sql.newprice;
```

```
                                    List
                 PRODUCT      COST  Price  LIST1990                       1
                 ------------------------------------
                 flippers      $16    $20       $24
                 jet ski   $2,150 $2,675    $3,210
                 kayak        $190   $240      $288
                 raft           $5     $7        $8
                 snorkel       $12    $15       $18
                 surfboard    $615   $750      $900
                 windsurfer $1,090 $1,325    $1,590
```

You can now use the ALTER statement to change the format of the columns.

```
alter table sql.newprice
   modify cost num format=dollar10.2,
          prodlist num format=dollar10.2,
          list1990 num format=dollar10.2;

select * from sql.newprice;
```

```
                 PRODUCT         COST  List Price    LIST1990              1
                 ---------------------------------------------------
                 flippers      $16.00      $20.00      $24.00
                 jet ski    $2,150.00   $2,675.00   $3,210.00
                 kayak        $190.00     $240.00     $288.00
                 raft           $5.00       $7.00       $8.40
                 snorkel       $12.00      $15.00      $18.00
                 surfboard    $615.00     $750.00     $900.00
                 windsurfer $1,090.00   $1,325.00   $1,590.00
```

---

* If you create the Newprice table with the previous example and then run this example, the second definition of the table overwrites the previous definition.

You can also use the ALTER statement to drop one or more columns from a table.

```
alter table sql.newprice
   drop cost;
```

```
select * from sql.newprice;
```

```
                                                                        1
      PRODUCT     List Price    LIST1990
      ---------------------------------------
      flippers         $20.00      $24.00
      jet ski      $2,675.00   $3,210.00
      kayak          $240.00     $288.00
      raft             $7.00       $8.40
      snorkel         $15.00      $18.00
      surfboard      $750.00     $900.00
      windsurfer   $1,325.00   $1,590.00
```

Updating Columns in a Table

In the example in the previous section, we used an ALTER statement to define a new column, LIST1990, for the Newprice table. When you display the first definition of this table, the new column has no values. The UPDATE statement adds or updates the values in a column in a table or the values in a column in a database management system (DBMS) table that is described by a SAS/ACCESS view. Notice that the ALTER statement defines a column while the UPDATE statement supplies or changes the data values in a column. These statements and their components are described in detail in Chapter 5.

The Newprice table and the LIST1990 column are defined as follows:

```
proc sql;
create table sql.newprice as
   select prodname as product, prodcost as cost,
          prodlist label='List Price'
       from sql.product;

alter table sql.newprice
   add list1990 num format=dollar.;
```

The UPDATE statement can use the values (and column attributes) in the PRODLIST column to create the values of the LIST1990 column. All the values in the LIST1990 column are updated because a WHERE expression is omitted.

```
update sql.newprice
   set list1990=prodlist*1.2;
```

```
select * from sql.newprice;
```

```
                                           1
                          List
       PRODUCT     COST   Price   LIST1990
       ------------------------------------
       flippers     $16    $20       $24
       jet ski   $2,150 $2,675    $3,210
       kayak       $190   $240      $288
       raft          $5     $7        $8
       snorkel      $12    $15       $18
       surfboard   $615   $750      $900
       windsurfer $1,090 $1,325   $1,590
```

If you want to update some, but not all, of a column's values, you can use a WHERE expression in the UPDATE statement. In the first UPDATE statement, the WHERE expression selects rows for the result table that have values less than or equal to 240 in the PRODLIST column. The first UPDATE example increases the list prices of the less expensive products, while the second UPDATE statement supplies values for products whose prices have not been changed by the first statement (that is, products costing more than $240).

```
update sql.newprice
   set list1990=prodlist*1.2
   where prodlist<=240;

update sql.newprice
   set list1990=prodlist
   where prodlist>240;

select * from sql.newprice;
```

```
                                           1
                          List
       PRODUCT     COST   Price   LIST1990
       ------------------------------------
       flippers     $16    $20       $24
       jet ski   $2,150 $2,675    $2,675
       kayak       $190   $240      $288
       raft          $5     $7        $8
       snorkel      $12    $15       $18
       surfboard   $615   $750      $750
       windsurfer $1,090 $1,325   $1,325
```

Alternatively, you can use a CASE expression as part of the SET clause to update all the LIST1990 values in one step. A CASE expression, which begins with the keyword CASE and ends with the keyword END, returns a single value that is evaluated conditionally for each row in the table.

In this example, the CASE expression selects the multiplier needed to return the 1990 list prices. For products costing less than or equal to 240, the multiplier is 1.2 (reflecting a 20% price increase); for products costing more than 240, the multiplier is 1, indicating no price change.

```
update sql.newprice
    set list1990=prodlist *
        case when prodlist<=240 then 1.2
             else 1
        end;


select * from sql.newprice;
```

```
                                    List
                  PRODUCT    COST   Price  LIST1990
                  ------------------------------------
                  flippers      $16     $20       $24
                  jet ski   $2,150  $2,675    $2,675
                  kayak        $190    $240      $288
                  raft           $5      $7        $8
                  snorkel       $12     $15       $18
                  surfboard    $615    $750      $750
                  windsurfer $1,090  $1,325    $1,325
```

To evaluate the first row of the Product table, for example, the CASE expression retrieves the PRODLIST price (20) for `flippers` and substitutes this number in the expression.

```
update sql.newprice
    set list1990=20 *
        case when 20<=240 then 1.2
             else 1
        end;
```

The CASE expression returns a single value—the list price of flippers as multiplied by 1.2—and this LIST1990 price is output in the result table as $24. The CASE expression then evaluates each subsequent row in the Product table and outputs their values.

Inserting Rows into a Table

The INSERT statement adds rows to a new or existing table, or it adds rows to a DBMS table described by a SAS/ACCESS view. Like the UPDATE statement, one form of the INSERT statement uses the SET clause. You can also use a VALUES clause or query-expression to insert a new row. A WHERE expression cannot be specified in an INSERT statement unless it is part of a query-expression. These statements and their components are described in detail in Chapter 5.

In the following Newprice table, a row is added using a SET clause. A SET clause is an sql-expression (described in Chapter 5) and can take a number of operands, including constants, as shown here.

```
proc sql;
create table sql.newprice as
    select prodname as product, prodcost as cost,
           prodlist label='List Price',
           (prodlist*1.2) as list1990 format=dollar.
        from sql.product;

insert into sql.newprice
    set product='umbrella',
        cost=12,
        prodlist=15,
        list1990=18;

select * from sql.newprice;
```

If you omit a column from the SET clause list, that column's value is set to NULL or MISSING.

```
                                         List                            1
              PRODUCT        COST      Price    LIST1990
              -------------------------------------------
              flippers       $16        $20        $24
              jet ski     $2,150     $2,675     $3,210
              kayak         $190       $240       $288
              raft            $5         $7         $8
              snorkel        $12        $15        $18
              surfboard     $615       $750       $900
              windsurfer  $1,090     $1,325     $1,590
              umbrella       $12        $15        $18
```

For the same result with fewer keystrokes, you can use the VALUES clause. The order of the values must match the order of the column names in the INSERT column list or, if no list is specified, the order of the columns in the table or SAS/ACCESS view. In this example, a column list is not included.

```
insert into sql.newprice
    values('umbrella',12,15,18);
```

If you do not specify an INSERT column list and omit a value from the VALUES clause list, an error message is written to the SAS log and no rows are inserted. If you specify an INSERT column list, accidently omit a column, but include a value for the omitted column in the VALUES clause list, the column's value is set to NULL or MISSING.

The last form of the INSERT statement uses a query-expression. This form is best used when you have a number of rows to add and do not want to type each column name and its value. It is also a way to move values into a table that are selected from another table.

Take the case, for example, when the wholesale company wants to introduce GT models of its rafts and kayaks. The GT models of these products cost the company 20% more than their base models, so the company plans to sell them for 30% more than the base price. The following example uses a query-expression to achieve the desired result:

```
proc sql undo_policy=none;
insert into sql.newprice
select trim(product) || " GT", cost*1.2 as cost,
       prodlist*1.3 as prodlist,
       list1990*1.3 as list1990
   from sql.newprice
   where product in ('raft','kayak');

select * from sql.newprice;
```

```
                                                                        1
                                  List
               PRODUCT     COST  Price  LIST1990
               ------------------------------------
               flippers     $16    $20       $24
               jet ski  $2,150 $2,675    $3,210
               kayak       $190   $240      $288
               raft          $5     $7        $8
               snorkel      $12    $15       $18
               surfboard   $615   $750      $900
               windsurfer $1,090 $1,325  $1,590
               umbrella     $12    $15       $18
               kayak GT    $228   $312      $374
               raft GT       $6     $9       $11
```

Deleting Rows from a Table

The DELETE statement enables you to delete one or all of the rows in a table or in a DBMS table mapped by a SAS/ACCESS view. This statement is described in detail in Chapter 5.

To delete the umbrella row from our sample table Newprice, use the following statement. The note is written to the SAS log.

```
proc sql;
delete
   from sql.newprice
   where product='umbrella';

NOTE:  1 row was deleted from SQL.NEWPRICE.
```

The DELETE statement should be used cautiously: if used without a WHERE expression, all the rows in your table are deleted.

Resetting SQL Procedure Options

The RESET statement enables you to add, drop, or change the options in the PROC SQL statement. You can list the options in any order in the PROC SQL and RESET statements.

This example first uses the NOPRINT option to prevent the SELECT statement from displaying its result table in SAS output. It then resets the

NOPRINT option to PRINT (the default) and adds the NUMBER option, which displays the row number in the result table.

```
proc sql noprint;
select * from sql.product;

reset print number;
select * from sql.product
   where prodcost<20;
```

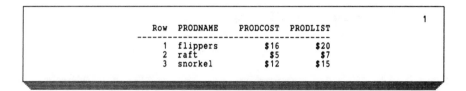

Options stay in effect until they are reset, so none of your result tables are displayed until you reset the SQL procedure using the PRINT option.

Chapter Summary

This chapter has introduced the ALTER, CREATE, DELETE, DESCRIBE, INSERT, RESET, and UPDATE statements and some of their clauses and components. It has covered the following topics:

□ creating and dropping tables, views, and indexes using the CREATE and DROP statements as well as describing view definitions using the DESCRIBE statement

□ modifying tables by adding, modifying, or dropping columns using the ALTER statement

□ adding and modifying data values in a table's columns using the UPDATE statement and inserting and deleting rows using the INSERT and DELETE statements

□ adding and resetting PROC SQL options using the RESET statement.

The next chapter shows you advanced features and uses of the SQL procedure. It also describes ways to improve query performance and some of the interfaces with which the SQL procedure works.

Chapter 4 Using the Advanced Features of the SQL Procedure

Introduction 59

Advanced Features of the SQL Procedure 59
Summary Functions and Remerging with the Data 60
Subqueries 63
Query-Expressions with Set Operators 64
Complex Joins 66
    Four-Way Joins 66
    Role of Indexes in Equijoins 69
    Outer Joins 71

Improving Query Performance 74
    Using Indexes to Improve Performance 74
    Using the Keyword ALL in Set Operations 74
    Omitting the ORDER BY Clause When Creating Tables and Views 75
    Using In-Line Views versus Temporary Tables 75
    Comparing Subqueries with Joins 75
    Using WHERE Expressions with Joins 75
Comparing Three Queries for Performance 76

SQL Procedure with Other SAS Interfaces 78
SAS/ACCESS Interface 79
Macro Facility Interface 81
Screen Control Language Interface 82

Chapter Summary 83

Introduction

This chapter shows you how to combine the SQL procedure statements and components to create powerful queries. It describes how you can use the SQL procedure with other SAS System features and interfaces to write more efficient programs.

Advanced Features of the SQL Procedure

The following descriptions and examples assume that you are familiar with the SQL procedure and the SAS System, and that you have read Chapter 5, "SQL Procedure." Refer to this chapter if you have questions about terms or want more information on the way a statement or component works.

Summary Functions and Remerging with the Data

A summary function produces a statistical summary of the data in an entire table or for groups in the table that are specified with the GROUP BY clause. These functions reduce the values in each column or row of a table to a single value; for example, the function SUM(EMPYEARS) adds all the values in the EMPYEARS column to produce a single result value. A summary function can appear in the SELECT or HAVING clauses. See "summary-function" in Chapter 5 for a list of the summary functions available under the SQL procedure and for more information on using them.

When a summary function is listed along with one or more arithmetic expressions or columns (variables) and those columns are not grouped using a GROUP BY clause, the results of the summary function are redistributed across the rows (that is, original data) of the source table. This action is called *remerging with the data.*

Using only one query to remerge the summarized values with the source data is a SAS System enhancement to SQL. In most versions of SQL, it takes two queries to get a remerged result: one query to compute the summary function's values for each group of the source table and another to remerge those values with the source data. The SQL procedure makes two passes through the data to accomplish these steps, so you only need to write and run one query. See "summary-function" in Chapter 5 for a description of the exact rules under which data are remerged.

The next three examples illustrate some cases in which a summary function causes or does not cause remerging. In this first example, a summary function is used alone in the SELECT clause, so it is evaluated without remerging with the data. This example computes the average number of years that all the employees have worked.

```
select avg(empyears) as avg
   from sql.employee;
```

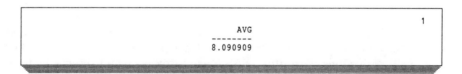

```
                                        1
                        AVG
                     --------
                     8.090909
```

In the next example, the column EMPTITLE is added to the SELECT list and a GROUP BY clause is added to the query that refers to this column. No data are remerged because you have associated an average-number-of-years value with each row of the GROUP BY item, EMPTITLE.

```
select emptitle, avg(empyears) as avg
   from sql.employee
   group by emptitle;
```

```
                                                          1
            EMPTITLE        AVG
            --------------------
            manager      9.666667
            president         28
            salesrep     4.571429
```

You can occasionally write queries that remerge data, with unexpected results. If the GROUP BY clause is omitted from the previous example, the average is calculated based on all the EMPYEARS (that is, EMPYEARS is treated as one group). The note is written to the SAS log.

```
select emptitle, avg(empyears) as avg
   from sql.employee;
```

```
NOTE: The query requires remerging summary statistics
      back with the original data.
```

```
                                                          1
            EMPTITLE        AVG
            --------------------
            president    8.090909
            manager      8.090909
            salesrep     8.090909
            salesrep     8.090909
            salesrep     8.090909
            salesrep     8.090909
            manager      8.090909
            salesrep     8.090909
            salesrep     8.090909
            manager      8.090909
            salesrep     8.090909
```

The statistic (8.090909) is remerged with the original data--the list of job titles--in the result table. While the query has performed correctly as specified, the results are misleading. The SQL procedure writes the note to the SAS log to let you know that remerging has occurred, in case you did not intend for it to do so.

The last example describes the two steps involved in remerging with the data in more detail. In this example, the president of the wholesale company wants to examine the invoices from each store in each chain of stores, for example, the invoices from each of the eight stores in the Coast Shop chain. Specifically, he wants to know the percentage that each invoice contributes to the chain's total sales.

```
proc sql;
select custname, custnum, invnum,
        (100*invqty*invprice)/sum(invqty*invprice) as percent
        format=9.6
    from  sql.invoice
    group by custname
    order by custname, percent desc;
```

In the SQL procedure's first pass through the data, it groups the rows in the Invoice table by their store chain and computes the SUM function. In the second pass through the data, it calculates the arithmetic expression for each row of the

Invoice table (100*INVQTY*INVPRICE) and divides that number (varying from row to row) by the results of the SUM function for each group (a constant value for each chain of stores), as shown in this internal table.

CUSTNAME	CUSTNUM	INVNUM	Expression	/ SUM per Chain
Beach Land	16	280	28000	705
Beach Land	16	290	28500	705
Beach Land	16	300	14000	705
Coast Shop	3	310	261000	4935
Coast Shop	3	320	18000	4935
Coast Shop	5	330	7500	4935
Coast Shop	5	340	28500	4935
Coast Shop	5	350	24000	4935
Coast Shop	5	360	15000	4935
Coast Shop	12	370	7000	4935
Coast Shop	14	380	132500	4935
Del Mar	3	390	54000	2105
Del Mar	3	400	69000	2105
Del Mar	8	410	24000	2105
Del Mar	11	420	10500	2105
Del Mar	11	430	15000	2105
Del Mar	11	440	38000	2105
New Waves	3	450	10000	3615
New Waves	3	460	20000	3615
New Waves	6	470	22500	3615
New Waves	6	480	294000	3615
New Waves	6	490	15000	3615
Surf Mart	101	500	28000	5250
Surf Mart	101	510	148000	5250
Surf Mart	101	520	18000	5250
Surf Mart	118	530	28500	5250
Surf Mart	118	540	18000	5250
Surf Mart	118	550	15000	5250
Surf Mart	127	560	47500	5250
Surf Mart	127	570	222000	5250

Thus, calculating the percentage for each row causes the results of the summary function to be remerged with the data from the Invoice table, as indicated by this message in the SAS log.

```
NOTE: The query requires remerging summary statistics
      back with the original data.
```

The final output table is sorted according to the chain's name and the percentage that each invoice contributes to the total, in descending order, as shown.

```
                                                                        1
            CUSTNAME    CUSTNUM   INVNUM    PERCENT
            ------------------------------------------
            Beach Land      16       290   40.425532
            Beach Land      16       280   39.716312
            Beach Land      16       300   19.858156
            Coast Shop       3       310   52.887538
            Coast Shop      14       380   26.849037
            Coast Shop       5       340    5.775076
            Coast Shop       5       350    4.863222
            Coast Shop       3       320    3.647416
            Coast Shop       5       360    3.039514
            Coast Shop       5       330    1.519757
            Coast Shop      12       370    1.418440
            Del Mar          3       400   32.779097
            Del Mar          3       390   25.653207
            Del Mar         11       440   18.052257
            Del Mar          8       410   11.401425
            Del Mar         11       430    7.125891
            Del Mar         11       420    4.988124
            New Waves        6       480   81.327801
            New Waves        6       470    6.224066
            New Waves        3       460    5.532503
            New Waves        6       490    4.149378
            New Waves        3       450    2.766252
            Surf Mart      127       570   42.285714
            Surf Mart      101       510   28.190476
            Surf Mart      127       560    9.047619
            Surf Mart      118       530    5.428571
            Surf Mart      101       500    5.333333
            Surf Mart      101       520    3.428571
            Surf Mart      118       540    3.428571
            Surf Mart      118       550    2.857143
```

For more information and examples on remerging, see "summary-function" and "having-expression" in Chapter 5.

Subqueries

Subqueries are introduced in Chapter 2, "Retrieving Data with the SELECT Statement." This section describes a more complex query that involves subqueries and other types of evaluations.

This example combines a number of components including summary functions, a HAVING expression with a subquery, and an in-line view within that subquery. The reason you use each component and the way in which it is evaluated are described following the example. This example displays the city with the greatest dollar sales.

```
proc sql;
select e.empcity, sum(invqty*invprice) as sales format=dollar.
    from sql.employee e, sql.invoice i
    where e.empnum=i.empnum
    group by empcity
    having sales=
            (select max(sales)
                from (select e.empcity, sum(invqty*invprice) as sales
                        from  sql.employee e, sql.invoice i
                        where e.empnum=i.empnum
                        group by empcity))
    order by 1;
```

As with any query that includes subqueries or in-line views, you begin evaluating the query at its innermost level. Here, the query begins by evaluating the in-line view, that is, the parenthesized SELECT expression in the FROM clause of the subquery in the HAVING clause.

The in-line view provides a list of the cities and the dollar amount sold in each city. You can then use this information to get the greatest dollar sales per city. The Employee and Invoice tables are joined over the EMPNUM column to get a list of the cities in which sales occurred and to use these sales figures to perform the SUM function.

```
       EMPCITY              SALES
    ---------------------------------
       Charleston           5370
       Myrtle Beach         4155
       Ocean City           1005
       Virgina Beach        3385
       Wilmington           2695
```

The SELECT MAX(SALES) clause uses the results of the in-line view to determine the highest sales amount, 5370. When this sales amount is supplied to the outer query, it evaluates as if it had been defined as follows:

```
select e.empcity, sum(invqty*invprice) as sales format=dollar.
   from sql.employee e, sql.invoice i
   where e.empnum=i.empnum
   group by empcity
   having sales=5370;
```

The first part of this query selects columns for the result table and joins the two tables over the matching employee numbers. The SUM function is then applied to the sales values for each city (that is, the group EMPCITY) and reduces the possible multiple rows for a city to one row. The HAVING expression then selects this row if it has the dollar sales amount 5370. The final result table with the formatted sales figure is as follows:

```
                                                              1
              EMPCITY        SALES
              ----------------------
              Charleston     $5,370
```

Query-Expressions with Set Operators

A query-expression with set operators is useful for listing the values derived from two or more table-expressions. The set operators supported by the SQL procedure are UNION, OUTER UNION, EXCEPT, and INTERSECT.

Queries with set operators remove duplicate rows by default unless the ALL keyword is specified. To eliminate duplicates, the SQL procedure makes another pass over the resulting data; this second pass has certain performance costs. If you know that there are no duplicate rows or if duplicate rows can remain in the result table, you should use the keyword ALL after the appropriate set operator.

This example uses the UNION operator to list products that were sold to stores in Myrtle Beach or sold by sales representatives who live in Virginia

Beach or both. Duplicate rows are automatically eliminated from the result table. For each row in the result table, the condition is listed that satisfies the query (using a constant from the SELECT list).

```
proc sql;
select 'Salesrep in Virginia Beach' as who, prodname as product
   from sql.invoice
   where 'Virginia Beach'=
         (select empcity
               from sql.employee
               where empnum=invoice.empnum)
union
select 'Store in Myrtle Beach' as who, prodname as product
   from sql.invoice
   where 'Myrtle Beach'=
         (select custcity
               from sql.customer
               where custname=invoice.custname and
                     custnum=invoice.custnum)
   order by 1, 2;
```

In this example, each table-expression (that is, SELECT expression) is evaluated separately, and their results are combined to produce this output.

```
                                                              1
      WHO                         PRODUCT
      ------------------------------------------------
      Salesrep in Virginia Beach  raft
      Salesrep in Virginia Beach  snorkel
      Salesrep in Virginia Beach  surfboard
      Store in Myrtle Beach       flippers
      Store in Myrtle Beach       raft
      Store in Myrtle Beach       snorkel
      Store in Myrtle Beach       windsurfer
```

This next example uses the EXCEPT operator to list the products that were sold by sales representatives who live in Virginia Beach, excluding those products sold to stores in Myrtle Beach.

```
select prodname as product
   from sql.invoice
   where 'Virginia Beach'=
         (select empcity
               from sql.employee
               where empnum=invoice.empnum)
except
select prodname as product
   from sql.invoice
   where 'Myrtle Beach'=
         (select custcity
               from sql.customer
               where custname=invoice.custname and
                     custnum=invoice.custnum)
   order by 1;
```

Again, each table-expression is evaluated separately, but here the difference between the two result tables is displayed.

```
                                                                    1

                         PRODUCT
                         ----------
                         surfboard
```

Complex Joins

Chapter 2 introduces joined tables and gives examples of how they are performed. This section shows you more complex joins, including outer joins and joins on four tables. For more information on joining tables and outer joins specifically, see "joined-table" in Chapter 5.

Four-Way Joins

This example shows how the SQL procedure performs a join on four tables (a four-way join). By selecting the order in which tables are processed internally, the SQL procedure can minimize the size of the query's intermediate tables. It does this by eliminating rows and columns from the intermediate tables as soon as they are no longer required by the remainder of the query, thus getting the query results more quickly.

The following query shows sales figures of items priced over $150 that were sold by each manager's group of sales representatives in the sample wholesale company. To get this result, you have to determine what information you need from which tables and how those tables need to be joined to get it. Take, for example, the Invoice table. Its entries reflect product sales but do not contain the cost of items (the query asks for items costing over $150); to get that data you need to join the Product table with the Invoice table. Also, its invoices are credited to the sales representative and not his or her manager, so you must connect the Invoice table to the Employee table through the sales representative's employee number. You can then join the Employee table with itself to obtain the manager data. An analysis of this query's evaluation follows the result table.

```
proc sql;
title 'Sales Figures';
select e1.empname as manager,
       count(i.invnum) as numsales,
       sum(i.invqty*i.invprice) as totsales,
       sum(i.invqty*p.prodcost) as totcost,
       sum(i.invqty*(i.invprice-p.prodcost)) as totmarg,
       sum(i.invqty*(i.invprice-p.prodcost))/
           sum(i.invqty*i.invprice) as pctmarg
    from sql.invoice i, sql.product p,
         sql.employee e1, sql.employee e2
    where i.prodname=p.prodname and p.prodcost>150 and
          i.empnum=e2.empnum and
          e1.emptitle='manager' and e1.empnum=e2.empboss
    group by manager;
```

```
                          Sales Figures                           1

    MANAGER   NUMSALES  TOTSALES   TOTCOST   TOTMARG   PCTMARG
    --------------------------------------------------------------
    Betty        1        2940      2460       480    0.163265
    Chuck        3        3495      2890       605    0.173104
    Sally        2        4830      4025       805    0.166667
```

When a join is evaluated, according to the *conceptual model,* it creates an internal or intermediate table that is the Cartesian product of all the tables in the join. For this query, the intermediate table would have 25,410 rows and 22 columns. This Cartesian product is then reduced to rows and columns that satisfy the WHERE expression and are requested by the SELECT clause. While an optimized SQL procedure processes this join more efficiently, it would get the same result if the join were processed according to this conceptual model.

The SQL procedure performs multiple (that is, on more than two tables) joins as a series of two-way joins, selecting pairs of tables to join in order to minimize the size of the intermediate tables to be constructed. In this query, it joins the Invoice and Product tables over the PRODNAME column first because, as an equijoin, this combination produces the smallest predicted result. (The WHERE expression of an equijoin has a condition in which the value of a column in the first table must equal the value of a column in the second.)

The Invoice and Product tables are joined over the PRODNAME column, thus satisfying the I.PRODNAME=P.PRODNAME condition in the WHERE expression. The product names, while not appearing in the result table (and therefore not in the intermediate table), are required so that you can determine which products were sold. The SQL procedure also restricts the number of rows output to items costing more than $150 (the second condition in the WHERE expression). It is more efficient and speeds processing to eliminate unneeded rows as soon as possible. This part of the four-way join would appear as follows if it were a separate two-way join:

```
create table t1 as
    select p.prodcost, i.empnum, i.invnum, i.invqty, i.invprice
        from sql.invoice i, sql.product p
        where i.prodname=p.prodname and p.prodcost>150;

title 'Intermediate Result T1';
select * from t1;
```

```
                  Intermediate Result T1

    PRODCOST    EMPNUM    INVNUM    INVQTY    INVPRICE
    ---------------------------------------------------

      $1,090      318       310        2       $1,305
      $1,090      417       380        1       $1,325
        $190      417       400        3         $230
        $615      213       480        4         $735
        $615      417       510        2         $740
        $615      314       570        3         $740
```

The EMPNUM column in table T1 represents the employee number of the person who made the sale, but for the purposes of this query, the sales representative's manager is needed. The SAS System gets this information by joining the intermediate table T1 with the Employee table over the EMPNUM column (the third condition in the original query's WHERE expression), retaining the column EMPBOSS; the EMPNUM column can be discarded once you get this manager information. This part of the four-way join would appear as follows if it were a separate two-way join:

```
create table t2 as
    select prodcost, empboss, invnum, invqty, invprice
        from t1, sql.employee e
        where t1.empnum=e.empnum;

title 'Intermediate Result T2';
select * from t2;
```

Intermediate Result T2

PRODCOST	EMPBOSS	INVNUM	INVQTY	INVPRICE
$1,090	301	310	2	$1,305
$1,090	401	380	1	$1,325
$190	401	400	3	$230
$615	201	480	4	$735
$615	401	510	2	$740
$615	301	570	3	$740

The final result table requires the managers' names, not their employee numbers. The SAS System gets this information by again joining the intermediate table T2 with the Employee table, matching EMPBOSS with EMPNUM in the Employee table and keeping the column EMPNAME; this process satisfies the fourth and fifth conditions in the original query's WHERE expression. The final output is limited to managers only, as requested. This part of the four-way join would appear as follows if it were a separate two-way join:

```
create table t3 as
    select prodcost, empname as manager, invnum, invqty, invprice
        from t2, sql.employee e
        where t2.empboss=e.empnum and e.emptitle='manager';

title 'Intermediate Result T3';
select * from t3;
```

Intermediate Result T3

PRODCOST	MANAGER	INVNUM	INVQTY	INVPRICE
$1,090	Sally	310	2	$1,305
$1,090	Chuck	380	1	$1,325
$190	Chuck	400	3	$230
$615	Betty	480	4	$735
$615	Chuck	510	2	$740
$615	Sally	570	3	$740

At this point, all the tables in the FROM clause have been evaluated, and the intermediate table T3 includes only those rows that satisfy all the conditions in the original query's WHERE expression. The SQL procedure can now group the data by MANAGER for the final output table and process the SELECT clause list for each group (that is, MANAGER).

```
title 'Final Result';
select manager,
       count(invnum) as numsales,
       sum(invqty*invprice) as totsales,
       sum(invqty*prodcost) as totcost,
       sum(invqty*(invprice-prodcost)) as totmarg,
       sum(invqty*(invprice-prodcost))/
           sum(invqty*invprice) as pctmarg
   from t3
   group by manager;
```

The final result table is repeated here for easy reference.

```
                        Final Result                          1

      MANAGER   NUMSALES   TOTSALES   TOTCOST   TOTMARG   PCTMARG
      --------------------------------------------------------------
      Betty        1         2940      2460       480     0.163265
      Chuck        3         3495      2890       605     0.173104
      Sally        2         4830      4025       805     0.166667
```

The order in which joins are processed is sensitive to the predicted size of each intermediate result table. For the original Sales Figures query, if there were many products or invoices, it would be more efficient to join the Employee table with itself so that the SQL procedure could use the EMPNUM column to get the managers' names. (The equijoin over the EMPNUM columns causes the tables to be sorted and merged according to the matching data values.) This result would then be joined to the result of the joined Invoice and Product tables. The SQL procedure automatically computes these alternatives each time it processes a query, adjusting to the predicted sizes of the tables as needed.

Role of Indexes in Equijoins

If tables do not have indexes defined on their columns, the SAS System processes equijoins by sorting the tables and merging the data according to the matching values. If an index is defined on one or more columns in a table participating in the equijoin, sorting is not required. (Sorting normally increases the total performance time, especially on large tables.) In this case, the SAS System performs a join by making a single pass over the unindexed table and looking up the data values in the index to find the matching rows in the indexed table.

The Sales Figures query (in the previous section) shows performance gains when indexes are defined on columns that participate in equijoins. The query can be run with the STIMER system option and the STIMER option in the PROC SQL statement so that you can get performance information about the query. See "Creating Indexes with the SQL Procedure" in Chapter 5 for more information on indexes.

When the Sales Figures query is run without indexes, the query is written to the SAS log with these and other statistics about the query's performance. (This query was run under the MVS/XA host system on an IBM computer; results will vary from system to system.)

```
NOTE: SQL Statement used the following resources:
     CPU time      - 00:00:00.30
     ...
```

When you define indexes on two columns in the Invoice table that are referenced in equijoins and run the query again, the query runs faster.

```
options stimer;
proc sql stimer;
create index empnum on sql.invoice(empnum);
create index prodname on sql.invoice(prodname);

title 'Sales Figures';
select e1.empname as manager,
       count(i.invnum) as numsales,
       sum(i.invqty*i.invprice) as totsales,
       sum(i.invqty*p.prodcost) as totcost,
       sum(i.invqty*(i.invprice-p.prodcost)) as totmarg,
       sum(i.invqty*(i.invprice-p.prodcost))/
           sum(i.invqty*i.invprice) as pctmarg
    from sql.invoice i, sql.product p,
         sql.employee e1, sql.employee e2
    where i.prodname=p.prodname and p.prodcost>150 and
          i.empnum=e2.empnum and
          e1.emptitle='manager' and e1.empnum=e2.empboss
    group by manager;
```

The query is again written to the SAS log with statistics about its performance. Even with this very small example, the performance gain was nearly 33% when indexes were used on the larger table's columns.

```
NOTE: SQL Statement used the following resources:
     CPU time      - 00:00:00.20
     ...
```

The next example shows that performance can be enhanced when indexes are defined on columns that participate in equijoins on a frequent basis. The more significant numbers are indicated in boldface. Again, the examples were run under the MVS/XA host system on an IBM computer; results will vary from system to system.

```
SAS LOG

COMMAND ===>

          data twoK; do i=1 to 2000; output; end; run;

NOTE: The data set WORK.TWOK has 2000 observations and 1 variable.
NOTE: DATA statement used the following resources:
      CPU time     - 00:00:00.10
      ...

          data fiftyK; do i=1 to 50000; output; end; run;

NOTE: The data set WORK.FIFTYK has 50000 observations and 1 variable.
NOTE: DATA statement used the following resources:
      CPU time     - 00:00:01.04
      ...

          options stimer;
          proc sql stimer;
          select count(*) from twoK t, fiftyK f where t.i=f.i;
NOTE: SQL Statement used the following resources:
      CPU time       - 00:00:06.75
      ...

          create unique index i on fiftyK(i);
NOTE: Single index I defined.
NOTE: SQL Statement used the following resources:
      CPU time     - 00:00:08.93
      ...

          select count(*) from twoK t, fiftyK f where t.i=f.i;
NOTE: SQL Statement used the following resources:
      CPU time       - 00:00:01.09
      ...
```

Thus, defining an index on the column in the larger table saved 5.66 seconds of CPU time, making the query run nearly six times faster than the one without an index.

Outer Joins

In the previous section and in Chapter 2, you have seen how the SQL procedure joins tables. A conventional join, or *inner join* as they are called, returns a result table for all the rows in a table that have one or more matching rows in the other table(s), as specified by the WHERE expression. This kind of join is the only one allowed by most SQL databases. However, the SQL procedure also provides *outer joins*, which further extend SQL's joining capabilities.

Outer joins are inner joins that have been augmented with rows that did not match with any from the other table in the join. Therefore, the result table includes rows that match and rows that do not match from the join's source tables. Outer joins can be performed on only two tables (or views) at a time.

A left outer join, for example, lists matching rows and adds one or more rows from the left-hand table that do not match with any row in the right-hand table. The ON clause replaces the WHERE expression of an inner join, although it serves the same purpose of selecting rows for output. In the following example, a left outer join is used to list all the products (based on the

PRODNAME match with the left-hand table PRODUCT) and sales of those products to the Beach Land store.

```
proc sql;
select p.prodname, i.invqty, i.invprice, p.prodlist,
       i.invqty*i.invprice format=dollar. label='Invoice Amount'
   from sql.product p left join sql.invoice i
   on p.prodname=i.prodname and i.custname='Beach Land';
```

This result table indicates that only two of the possible seven products were sold to the Beach Land store.

```
                                                Invoice       1
         PRODNAME    INVQTY  INVPRICE  PRODLIST  Amount
         ------------------------------------------------
         flippers      15      $19       $20     $285
         jet ski        .        .    $2,675       .
         kayak          .        .      $240       .
         raft          20       $7        $7     $140
         snorkel       20      $14       $15     $280
         surfboard      .        .      $750       .
         windsurfer     .        .    $1,325       .
```

A standard, inner join could not be used here because it would list only the products sold to the Beach Land store instead of all the products sold, including those to Beach Land.

The next example uses DATA steps to create four tables and the SQL procedure to perform a full outer join on them. A full outer join displays all the rows in the Cartesian product of the tables where the sql-expression (in the ON clause) is satisfied, plus row(s) from each table that do not match with any row in any other table. The COALESCE function returns the first argument whose value is not a SAS missing value. See "sql-expression" in Chapter 5 for more information on the COALESCE function.

```
data j1;
   input x1 j1$;
   cards;
0 j1_0
1 j1_1
;

data j2;
   input x2 j2$;
   cards;
0 j2_0
2 j2_2
;

data j3;
   input x3 j3$;
   cards;
0 j3_0
3 j3_3
;
```

```
data j4;
   input x4 j4$;
   cards;
0 j4_0
4 j4_4
;

proc sql;
title 'Example One';
select coalesce(x1,x2,x3,x4) as x,j1,j2,j3,j4
   from j1 full join j2 on x1=x2
           full join j3 on x1=x3
           full join j4 on x1=x4;

title 'Ordered Example One';
select coalesce(x1,x2,x3,x4) as x,j1,j2,j3,j4
   from j1 full join j2 on x1=x2
           full join j3 on x1=x3
           full join j4 on x1=x4
order by 1;
```

The first SELECT statement displays the result table in a system-defined order (see "Sorting the Results (ORDER BY Clause)" in Chapter 2 for more information on system-defined ordering). The SQL procedure has evaluated the four-way join as a series of two-way joins and the order of the output reflects this process. The second SELECT statement includes an ORDER BY clause, so it is ordered as specified. See "joined-table" in Chapter 5 and "Four-Way Joins" earlier in this chapter for more information on complex joins.

```
                         Example One                            1

           X   J1          J2          J3          J4
           ---------------------------------------------------
           2               j2_2
           3                           j3_3
           0   j1_0        j2_0        j3_0        j4_0
           1   j1_1
           4                                       j4_4


                      Ordered Example One                       2

           X   J1          J2          J3          J4
           ---------------------------------------------------
           0   j1_0        j2_0        j3_0        j4_0
           1   j1_1
           2               j2_2
           3                           j3_3
           4                                       j4_4
```

If an inner join were performed on the four tables, only the row with the value of 0 for X would be returned, because it is the only row that satisfies the expressions in the ON clause across all the tables.

Improving Query Performance

The following sections give you general guidelines and specific situations to show how you can improve the performance of your SQL procedure queries. The sections are listed by topic. See also the full descriptions of the topics in Chapter 5.

Using Indexes to Improve Performance

Indexes are created with the CREATE INDEX statement in the SQL procedure or alternatively with the MODIFY and INDEX CREATE statements in the DATASETS procedure. Indexes are stored in specialized members of a SAS data library and have a SAS member type of INDEX. The values stored in an index are automatically updated if you make a change to the underlying data.

Indexes can improve the performance of certain classes of retrievals. For example, if an indexed column is compared to a constant value in a WHERE expression, the index will improve the query's performance. Indexing the column specified in a correlated reference to an outer table also improves a subquery's (and hence, query's) performance.

Composite indexes can improve the performance of queries that compare the columns named in the composite index with constant values that are linked using the AND operator. For example, if you have a compound index on the columns CITY and STATE and the WHERE expression is specified as WHERE CITY='xxx' AND STATE='yy', the index can be used to select that subset of rows more efficiently.

Indexes can also benefit queries that have a WHERE clause of the form

```
... where var1 in (select item1 from table1) ...
```

The values of VAR1 from the outer query are looked up in the inner query using the index.

An index can improve the processing of a table join, if the columns that participate in the join are indexed in one of the tables. This optimization can only be done for equijoin queries, that is, when the WHERE expression specifies that *table1.x=table2.y*. See "Creating Indexes with the SQL Procedure" in Chapter 5 for more information on indexes. See also "SAS Indexes" in Chapter 6, "SAS Files," of *SAS Language: Reference, Version 6, First Edition* for a description of creating and managing indexes.

Using the Keyword ALL in Set Operations

Set operators, such as UNION, OUTER UNION, EXCEPT, and INTERSECT, can be used in query-expressions to link tables together. See "query-expression" in Chapter 5 for more information on the individual set operators.

Specifying the optional ALL keyword prevents the final process that eliminates duplicate rows from the result table. You should use the ALL form when you know there are no duplicate rows or when it does not matter if the duplicate rows remain in the result table.

Omitting the ORDER BY Clause When Creating Tables and Views

You can use the ORDER BY clause to sort your table or view's output. If you specify the ORDER BY clause when a table or view is created, the data are always displayed in that order unless you specify another ORDER BY clause in a query that references that table or view. As with any kind of sorting procedure, using ORDER BY when retrieving data has certain performance costs, especially on large tables. If your output's order is not important for your results, your queries will run faster without an ORDER BY clause.

Using In-Line Views versus Temporary Tables

It is often helpful when you are exploring a problem to break a query down into several steps and create temporary tables to hold the intermediate results. Once you have worked through the problem, combining the queries into one query using in-line views is more efficient. This situation is especially true if the query is to be run a number of times. The SQL procedure does not optimize between two queries (or SQL statements), but it can often access data more efficiently when you specify one query that contains in-line views.

Comparing Subqueries with Joins

Many subqueries can also be expressed as joins. In general, the joined form is processed at least as efficiently as the subquery. The SQL procedure stores the result values for each unique set of correlation columns temporarily, thereby eliminating the need to calculate the subquery more than once.

Using WHERE Expressions with Joins

When joining tables, you should specify a WHERE expression. Joins without WHERE expressions are often time-consuming to evaluate because of the multiplier effect of the Cartesian product. For example, joining two tables of 1000 rows each, without specifying a WHERE expression or an ON clause, produces a result table with 1 million rows.

The SQL procedure executes and obtains the correct results on unbalanced WHERE expressions (or ON join-expressions) in an equijoin, as shown here, but handles them inefficiently.

```
where table1.columnA-table2.columnB=0
```

It is more efficient to rewrite this clause to balance the expression so that columns from each table are on alternate sides of the equals condition.

```
where table1.columnA=table2.columnB
```

The SQL procedure processes joins that do not have an equijoin condition in a sequential fashion, evaluating each row against the WHERE expression: that is, joins without an equijoin condition are not evaluated using sort-merge or index-lookup techniques.

Evaluating left and right outer joins is generally comparable to, or only slightly slower than, a standard inner join. A full outer join usually requires two passes over both tables in the join, although the SQL procedure tries to store as much data as possible in buffers; thus for small tables, an outer join may be processed with only one physical read of the data.

Comparing Three Queries for Performance

There is often more than one way to write a query to get the same information. Generally, the simpler a query, the faster it runs and the fewer resources it uses. While subqueries, in-line views, and joins give you more information, they can also take longer to process than a simple retrieval of data from one table. For example, each of the following queries lists the customers who have the greatest number of stores:

```
proc sql;
title 'Query One';
select distinct custname
   from sql.customer c1
   where (select count(*)
             from sql.customer c2
             where c2.custname=c1.custname)
       =
         (select max(numstore)
             from (select count(*) as numstore
                      from sql.customer
                      group by custname))
     order by 1;
```

```
                          Query One                          1

                          CUSTNAME
                          ----------
                          Coast Shop
                          Surf Mart
```

This query lists the customers with the greatest number of stores and how many stores each of them has.

```
title 'Query Two';
select distinct custname, count(*)
   from sql.customer c1
   group by custname
   having count(*)=
          (select max(numstore)
              from (select count(*) as numstore
                       from sql.customer
                       group by custname))
     order by 1;
```

```
                          Query Two                          1

             CUSTNAME
             --------------------
             Coast Shop            4
             Surf Mart            4
```

Query Two uses less CPU time than Query One (.010 of a CPU second compared with .016) and provides more information by listing the number of stores. Query One compares a correlated subquery with a subquery that includes an in-line view in the WHERE expression. Query Two uses one subquery with an in-line view as the predicate in the HAVING expression.

Another way to get this information is to create a simple, temporary table and perform a query on it. Doing so divides the query into two steps: the TEMP table lists all the customers and the number of stores each has; the SELECT statement then chooses the customers who have the most stores.

```
proc sql stimer;
title 'Query Three';
create table temp as
    select custname, count(*) as numstore
        from sql.customer
        group by custname;

select distinct custname, numstore
    from temp
    where numstore=
            (select max(numstore)
                from temp)
    order by 1;

reset nostimer;
```

```
                          Query Three                        1

             CUSTNAME    NUMSTORE
             --------------------
             Coast Shop           4
             Surf Mart            4
```

Query Three requires slightly more CPU time than Query Two: .012 versus .010 of a CPU second, running under MVS/XA on an IBM computer. You can choose either one to list the customers with the greatest number of stores. However, as noted earlier in "Improving Query Performance," the SQL procedure cannot optimize between two queries (or SQL statements) but can often do so within one query. Therefore, Query Two performs the best of the three examples.

To get information about how your host system uses resources, you can use the STIMER system option when you invoke the SAS System. This option gives you a listing in the SAS log of the resources used for the entire procedure execution. If you also specify the PROC SQL option STIMER, you get a query-by-query listing in the SAS log of the resources used. You can use the RESET statement after the query to turn off the PROC SQL STIMER option.

The following display lists part of the SAS log contents for Query Three. In this example, the STIMER system option was specified when the SAS System was invoked. The PROC SQL STIMER option has also been specified in this example. This SAS log was created on an IBM computer running under the MVS/XA host system; the actual figures will vary from system to system.

```
SAS LOG

COMMAND ===>

130     title 'Query Three';
NOTE: PROCEDURE SQL used the following resources:
      CPU time      - 00:00:00.07
      Elapsed time - 00:02:22.54
      EXCP count    - 3
      Task  memory - 1136K (20K data, 1116K program)
      Total memory - 4127K (2084K data, 2043K program)

131     proc sql stimer;
NOTE: SQL Statement used the following resources:
      CPU time      - 00:00:00.03
      Elapsed time - 00:00:00.37
      EXCP count    - 0
      Task  memory - 469K (20K data, 449K program)
      Total memory - 4127K (2084K data, 2043K program)
132     create table temp as
133     select custname, count(*) as numstore
134       from sql.customer
135       group by custname;
NOTE: Table WORK.TEMP created, with 6 rows and 2 columns.

NOTE: SQL Statement used the following resources:
      CPU time      - 00:00:00.06
      Elapsed time - 00:00:03.83
      EXCP count    - 32
      Task  memory - 1014K (68K data, 946K program)
      Total memory - 4325K (2148K data, 2177K program)
136
137     select distinct custname, numstore
138       from temp
139       where numstore =
140               (select max(numstore)
141                  from temp)
142       order by 1;
NOTE: SQL Statement used the following resources:
      CPU time      - 00:00:00.06
      Elapsed time - 00:00:01.47
      EXCP count    - 4
      Task  memory - 1265K (200K data, 1065K program)
      Total memory - 4453K (2276K data, 2177K program)
143
144     reset nostimer;
```

SQL Procedure with Other SAS Interfaces

The SQL procedure also operates with the SAS/ACCESS, macro facility, and the Screen Control Language (SCL) interfaces. For more information on these products, see "Using This Book" for a list of their usage guides.

SAS/ACCESS Interface

The *SAS/ACCESS software* provides an interface between the SAS System and an external database management system (DBMS), such as IBM's DB2™ or Digital Equipment Corporation's VAX™ Rdb/VMS™ This interface enables you to access DBMS data directly and use them in SAS programs; that is, you no longer have to extract the DBMS data first and place them in a SAS data file before you can use the data in a SAS program. The interface also enables you to update a DBMS table from within a SAS program and to create and load DBMS tables with data from SAS data files or views created with the SQL and ACCESS procedures.

This section uses the SAS/ACCESS interface to DB2 in its examples. The DB2 sample database concerns a fictional company that sells products worldwide for medical and scientific research. The first query displays data described by the SAS/ACCESS view (or view descriptor) DB2V.CUSPHONE. This view describes a subset of data from the DB2 table CUSTOMERS. The OPTIONS statement sets the output width to 120 characters.

```
options linesize=120;
proc sql;
title 'Data Described by DB2V.CUSPHONE';
select * from db2v.cusphone;
```

The CUSTOMER number identifies where the customer company is located, for example, all numbers beginning with 1 mean that the customer lives in the United States. The NAME and TELEPHONE columns give the customer's name and telephone number, respectively.

```
                          Data Described by DB2V.CUSPHONE

CUSTOMER  TELEPHONE     NAME
-----------------------------------------------------------------------------------------
12345678  919/489-5682
14324742  408/629-0589  SANTA CLARA VALLEY TECHNOLOGY SPECIALISTS
14569877  919/489-6792  PRECISION PRODUCTS
14898029  301/760-2541  UNIVERSITY BIOMEDICAL MATERIALS
15432147  616/582-3906  GREAT LAKES LABORATORY EQUIPMENT MANUFACTURERS
18543489  512/478-0788  LONE STAR STATE RESEARCH SUPPLIERS
19783482  703/714-2900  TWENTY-FIRST CENTURY MATERIALS
19876078  209/686-3953  SAN JOAQUIN SCIENTIFIC AND INDUSTRIAL SUPPLY, INC.
24589689  (012)736-202  CENTAR ZA TECHNICKU I NAUCNU RESTAURIRANJE UMJETNINA
26422096    4268-54-72  SOCIETE DE RECHERCHES POUR DE CHIRURGIE ORTHOPEDIQUE
26984578      43-57-04  INSTITUT FUR TEXTIL-FORSCHUNGS
27654351   02/215-37-32 INSTITUT DE RECHERCHE SCIENTIFIQUE MEDICALE
28710427   (021)570517  ANTONIE VAN LEEUWENHOEK VERENIGING VOOR MICROBIOLOGIE
29834248   (0552)715311 BRITISH MEDICAL RESEARCH AND SURGICAL SUPPLY
31548901  406/422-3413  NATIONAL COUNCIL FOR MATERIALS RESEARCH
38763919      244-6324  INSTITUTO DE BIOLOGIA Y MEDICINA NUCLEAR
39045213  012/302-1021  LABORATORIO DE PESQUISAS VETERNINARIAS DESIDERIO FINAMOR
43290587   (02)933-3212 HASSEI SAIBO GAKKAI
43459747   03/734-5111  RESEARCH OUTFITTERS
46543295   (03)022-2332 WESTERN TECHNOLOGICAL SUPPLY
46783280       3762855  NGEE TECHNOLOGICAL INSTITUTE
48345514        213445  GULF SCIENTIFIC SUPPLIES
```

DB2 is a trademark of International Business Machines Corporation.

VAX and Rdb/VMS are trademarks of Digital Equipment Corporation.

The second query displays data described by the SAS/ACCESS view DB2V.CUSORDER. This view describes a subset of data from the DB2 table ORDERS.

```
options linesize=76;
proc sql;
title 'Data Described by DB2V.CUSORDER';
select * from db2v.cusorder;
```

The STOCKNUM column gives the stock number of a product sent to SHIPTO, which corresponds with the CUSTOMER column in the CUSTOMERS table.

```
                 Data Described by DB2V.CUSORDER

                      STOCKNUM  SHIPTO
                      ------------------
                          9870  19876078
                          1279  39045213
                          8934  18543489
                          3478  29834248
                          2567  19783482
                          4789  15432147
                          3478  29834248
                          1279  14324742
                          8934  31548901
                          2567  14898029
                          9870  48345514
                          1279  39045213
                          8934  18543489
                          2567  19783482
                          9870  18543489
                          3478  24589689
                          1279  38763919
                          8934  43459747
                          2567  15432147
                          9870  14324742
                          9870  19876078
                          1279  39045213
                          8934  18543489
                          3478  29834248
                          2567  19783482
                          4789  15432147
                          3478  29834248
                          1279  14324742
                          8934  31548901
                          2567  14898029
                          9870  48345514
                          1279  39045213
                          8934  18543489
                          2567  19783482
                          9870  18543489
                          3478  24589689
                          1279  38763919
                          8934  43459747
                          2567  15432147
                          9870  14324742
```

The data in these two views are joined so that information about USA customers who have ordered gold (STOCKNUM 8934) is displayed.

```
title 'USA Customers Who Ordered Gold';
select distinct customer, name
   from db2v.cusphone, db2v.cusorder
   where customer=shipto and customer like '1%'
         and stocknum=8934;
```

```
                        USA Customers Who Ordered Gold
             CUSTOMER  NAME
             ---------------------------------------------------
             18543489  LONE STAR STATE RESEARCH SUPPLIERS
```

You can also use the SQL procedure to update a DBMS table or a DBMS table underlying a DBMS view. On the other hand, the data from a table or view created by PROC SQL can be loaded into a DBMS table. See the SAS/ACCESS interface for your database management system for more information.

Macro Facility Interface

The macro facility is a programming tool for extending and customizing SAS software and for reducing the amount of text you must enter to do common tasks. You can use the macro facility with the SQL procedure, as shown in the next example.

This example creates a table listing people who are qualified to serve as referees for a review of academic papers. No more than three people per subject are allowed in a table. The SAS macro language is used to check the count of those people qualified to referee a subject before inserting a new person.

Once you have created the Referee table, you can define a SAS macro to insert people's names into the table. The macro has two parameters: the person's name and the subject for which he is qualified to referee.

```
proc sql;
create table sql.referee
        (name     char(15),
         subject char(15));

%macro  addref(name,subject);
%local count;

    /* Do we have three people who can referee this subject? */
  reset noprint;
  select count(*)
      into :count
      from sql.referee
      where subject="&subject";

%if &count>=3 %then %do;
    reset print;
    title  "ERROR: &name not inserted for subject - &subject..";
    title2 "      There are 3 referees already.";
    select * from sql.referee where subject="&subject";
    reset noprint;
    %end;

%else %do;
    insert into sql.referee(name,subject) values("&name","&subject");
    %put NOTE: &name has been added for subject - &subject..;
    %end;
```

```
%mend;

%addref(Conner,sailing);
%addref(Fay,sailing);
%addref(Einstein,relativity);
%addref(Smythe,sailing);
%addref(Naish,sailing);
```

Submitting the %ADDREF() macros adds referee names to the table. While this method does not prevent a user from coding his or her own INSERT statements, this macro may be suitably secure if embedded in an application. A note appears in the SAS log once each macro has executed, as shown here.

```
SAS LOG

COMMAND ===>

33      %addref(Conner,sailing);
NOTE: Conner has been added for subject - sailing.
34      %addref(Fay,sailing);
NOTE: Fay has been added for subject - sailing.
35      %addref(Einstein,relativity);
NOTE: Einstein has been added for subject - relativity.
36      %addref(Smythe,sailing);
NOTE: Smythe has been added for subject - sailing.
37      %addref(Naish,sailing);
```

The result table has a row added with each execution of the %ADDREF macro. When the table contains three referees, it is displayed in SAS output with the message that it can accept no more referees.

```
            ERROR: Naish not inserted for subject - sailing.          1
                   There are 3 referees already.

            NAME          SUBJECT
            --------------------------------
            Conner        sailing
            Fay           sailing
            Smythe        sailing
```

Screen Control Language Interface

The Screen Control Language (SCL) is a programming language that is available in SAS/AF and SAS/FSP software. SCL provides functions and routines for managing applications and their windows and for controlling the application's environment.

The Referee table created in the preceding macro facility example can be used in this SCL example. In this case, the INSERT statements are processed from a SAS/AF application.

Here the example assumes you have built your primary menu and are using SCL to write the source portion of your program entry. The SAS/AF SOURCE window is designed with two fields, name and subject. The program associated with the window is as follows:

```
INIT:
   control always;
   return;

MAIN:
   submit continue sql;
      /* Do we already have three people who can do this subject? */
   reset noprint;
   select count(*)
      into :count
      from sql.referee
      where subject="&subject";
   endsubmit;

   if symget('count')>=3 then
      _msg_ = 'ERROR: ' || trim(name) || ' not inserted.';

   else do;
      submit continue sql;
         insert into sql.referee values("&name","&subject");
      endsubmit;
      _msg_ = 'NOTE: ' || trim(name) || ' has been added for '
               || subject;
   end;

TERM:
   return;
```

Chapter Summary

This chapter has analyzed some complex examples with subqueries, set operations, four-table joins, and statistical summary. It has described ways to improve query performance. The SQL procedure's interfaces with the SAS/ACCESS software, the macro facility, and the Screen Control Language were also illustrated.

The next chapter serves as a reference guide for the SQL procedure and explains all of its options, statements, and components.

Part 3

Reference Guide for the SQL Procedure

Chapter 5   **SQL Procedure**

Chapter **5** SQL Procedure

Overview 88

Syntax 88
SQL Procedure Coding Conventions 89
PROC SQL and RESET Statements 89
SQL Procedure and SAS Data Set Options 92

Statements in the SQL Procedure 95
    ALTER Statement 95
    CREATE Statement 97
    DELETE Statement 104
    DESCRIBE Statement 105
    DROP Statement 107
    INSERT Statement 108
    SELECT Statement 112
    UPDATE Statement 114
    VALIDATE Statement 117

Macro Variables Set by Statements in the SQL Procedure 118

Components of the SQL Procedure Statements 120
    between-condition 120
    case-expression 121
    column-definition 123
    column-modifier 125
    column-name 127
    exists-condition 129
    from-list 130
    group-by-item 132
    having-expression 134
    host-variable 137
    in-condition 139
    is-condition 140
    joined-table 142
    like-condition 147
    object-item 149
    order-by-item 151
    query-expression 152
    set-clause 159
    sql-expression 161
    summary-function 169
    table-expression 175
    table-name 176
    values-clause 178
    where-expression 179

Chapter Summary 181

Overview

The SQL procedure uses the Structured Query Language (SQL) to create, modify, and retrieve data from tables and views. In this book, a table is a SAS data file and a PROC SQL view is derived from one or more tables or other views. The term *SAS data view* is used when either a PROC SQL or SAS/ACCESS view can be referenced in an SQL statement.

This chapter describes the SQL procedure and its options, statements, and language components. The Structured Query Language is a modular type of language, in that queries (or statements) are composed of smaller building blocks called *components*. This chapter is organized to reflect these components, describing the statements that PROC SQL processes and then listing (in alphabetical order) the components that constitute these statements.

Refer to *SAS Language: Reference, Version 6, First Edition* for more information on SAS data sets and data libraries and their naming conventions or for help with the terminology used in this procedure description.

Refer to Chapter 2, "Retrieving Data with the SELECT Statement," and Chapter 3, "Creating and Modifying Tables and Views," for more examples of how to use the SQL procedure statements and components described in this chapter.

Syntax

The SQL procedure includes several statements, two of which can take options:

PROC SQL <*option* <*option*>... >;

ALTER *alter-statement*;
CREATE *create-statement*;
DELETE *delete-statement*;
DESCRIBE *describe-statement*;
DROP *drop-statement*;
INSERT *insert-statement*;
RESET <*option* <*option*>... >;
SELECT *select-statement*;
UPDATE *update-statement*;
VALIDATE *validate-statement*;

SQL Procedure Coding Conventions

Because the SQL procedure implements the Structured Query Language, it works somewhat differently than other base SAS procedures, as described here:

□ You do not need to repeat the PROC statement with each query or SQL statement. You only need to repeat it if you process a DATA step or another SAS procedure between queries.

□ SQL procedure statements are divided into clauses, for example, the most basic SELECT statement contains the SELECT and FROM clauses. Items within SQL clauses are separated with commas, not blanks, as in the SAS System. For example, if you list three columns in the SELECT clause, the columns are separated with commas.

□ The SELECT statement, used to retrieve data, also outputs the data automatically unless you specify the NOPRINT option in the PROC SQL statement. Thus, you can display your output or send it to a list file without specifying the PRINT procedure.

□ The SELECT and CREATE VIEW statements can each include an ORDER BY clause that enables you to sort data by columns, so you do not need to use the SORT procedure with your PROC SQL programs. SAS data sets do not need to be presorted by a variable for use in the SQL procedure.

□ A PROC SQL statement runs without a RUN statement. If you follow a PROC SQL statement with a RUN statement, the SAS System will just ignore the RUN statement and execute the statements as usual.

See the descriptions and examples of each SQL procedure statement later in this chapter for more information.

PROC SQL and RESET Statements

PROC SQL and RESET statements have the following form:

PROC SQL <*option* <*option*>... >;
RESET < *option* <*option*>... >;

The following options can appear in the PROC SQL statement or the RESET statement. Used in the PROC SQL statement, they specify the initial state of an option. Options can be added, removed, or changed between PROC SQL statements by means of the RESET statement. An option remains in effect until its NO version is specified (for example, NOEXEC) or until it is reset.

Options must be typed exactly as shown. The options are as follows:

ERRORSTOP | NOERRORSTOP
specifies whether the SAS System should stop processing if an error is encountered. If the EXEC option is in effect, the SAS System always checks the PROC SQL syntax for accuracy and, if no error occurs, executes the SQL statement.

Specifying ERRORSTOP instructs the SAS System to continue checking the syntax once it has encountered an error in processing a PROC SQL statement in a SAS batch or noninteractive job. However, it stops executing the SQL procedure statements after the error.

(ERRORSTOP continued)

ERRORSTOP only has an effect when the SAS System is running in the batch and noninteractive execution modes.

NOERRORSTOP is the default in an interactive SAS session, but it works with all the execution modes. Resetting NOERRORSTOP to ERRORSTOP during an interactive session works only if you also reset the EXEC option to NOEXEC. See also the NOEXEC option.

Specifying NOERRORSTOP instructs the SAS System to continue checking the syntax of SQL statements after an error occurs. It continues to try to execute the statements if the EXEC option is in effect. NOERRORSTOP is useful if you want a batch job to continue processing PROC SQL statements after an error has been encountered.

EXEC | NOEXEC

specifies whether a statement should be executed after its syntax is checked for accuracy. EXEC is the default. See the ERRORSTOP option for the ways in which the two options interact.

NOEXEC is the only option that controls SQL statements that are run during an interactive SAS session. NOEXEC is useful if you want to check only the syntax of your SQL code without having the statements execute.

FEEDBACK | NOFEEDBACK

requests that the procedure display the query after it has expanded view references or made certain transformations on the query. NOFEEDBACK is the default.

This option expands any use of an asterisk (for example, SELECT *) into the list of qualified columns it represents. Any PROC SQL view is expanded into the underlying query and all expressions are fully parenthesized to further indicate their order of evaluation. See "Examples" following this section and the "DESCRIBE Statement" for more information on this option.

INOBS=*n*

restricts the number of rows (observations) that PROC SQL processes from any single source. For example, if you had specified INOBS=10 and were joining two tables without using a WHERE clause, you would get a maximum of 100 rows in the output. This option is useful for debugging queries on large tables.

LOOPS=*n*

requests that the procedure limit itself to *n* iterations through its inner loop. You can use the number of iterations reported in the SQLOOPS macro variable (after each SQL statement is executed) to gauge this value. Setting a limit prevents queries from consuming excessive computer resources. For example, joining three large tables without meeting the join-matching conditions could create a huge internal table that would be quite inefficient to process; using the LOOPS option can prevent this sort of error. For more information on loops, see "Macro Variables Set by Statements in the SQL Procedure" later in this chapter.

NUMBER | NONUMBER

specifies whether the SELECT statement should include a column called ROW, which is the row (or observation) number of the data as they are retrieved. This option works like the NOOBS option in the PRINT procedure. NONUMBER is the default.

OUTOBS=*n*

restricts the number of rows (or observations) that PROC SQL processes as the target of an SQL statement. For example, if you specify OUTOBS=10 and insert values into a table using a query-expression, PROC SQL inserts a maximum of ten rows.

PRINT | NOPRINT

specifies whether a SELECT statement's results are printed (that is, displayed) in SAS output. PRINT is the default. The NOPRINT option is useful when you are selecting values from a table into macro variables and do not want anything to be displayed.

SORTSEQ=*sort-tablename*

specifies the collating sequence to be used when a query contains an ORDER BY clause. Use this option only if you want a collating sequence other than your system's or installation's default collating sequence. For more information, see the SORTSEQ= option under the SORT procedure in the *SAS Procedures Guide, Version 6, Third Edition.*

STIMER | NOSTIMER

specifies whether the procedure writes (to the SAS log) timing information for each statement, rather than as a cumulative value for the entire procedure. For this option to work, the SAS system option STIMER must also be specified. Some host systems require you to specify the SAS system option STIMER when you invoke the SAS System. If you use the system option alone, you will get timing information for the entire procedure, not on each statement in the query. NOSTIMER is the default.

Examples

These statements create and retrieve data using the Highqty view definition. The view's SELECT statement lists all the invoices that show sales of 25 or more items. The note is written to the SAS log.

```
proc sql;
create view sql.highqty as
   select *
   from sql.invoice
   where invqty>=25;

NOTE:  SQL view SQL.HIGHQTY has been defined.

reset feedback;
select * from sql.highqty;
```

The RESET statement resets the PROC SQL statement and, in this case, enables you to add a new option. When you use the FEEDBACK option, your view's definition appears in the SAS log in an expanded form; that is, the FROM clause includes the entire query that composes the referenced view.

```
SAS LOG

COMMAND ===>

NOTE: Statement transforms to:

        select INVOICE.INVNUM, INVOICE.CUSTNAME, INVOICE.CUSTNUM,
INVOICE.EMPNUM, INVOICE.PRODNAME, INVOICE.INVQTY, INVOICE.INVPRICE
          from ( select INVOICE.INVNUM, INVOICE.CUSTNAME,
INVOICE.CUSTNUM, INVOICE.EMPNUM, INVOICE.PRODNAME, INVOICE.INVQTY,
INVOICE.INVPRICE
                 from SQL.INVOICE
                 where INVOICE.INVQTY >= 25 );
```

The result table is displayed in SAS output.

```
                                                                 1
     INVNUM  CUSTNAME     CUSTNUM   EMPNUM  PRODNAME    INVQTY  INVPRICE
    ------------------------------------------------------------------
        320  Coast Shop      3       318   raft          30       $6
        350  Coast Shop      5       318   raft          40       $6
        390  Del Mar         3       417   flippers      30      $18
        410  Del Mar         8       417   raft          40       $6
        540  Surf Mart     118       318   raft          30       $6
        560  Surf Mart     127       314   flippers      25      $19
```

You can also use the DESCRIBE statement to display a view definition. See its description later in this chapter.

SQL Procedure and SAS Data Set Options

The SQL procedure can apply most of the SAS data set options, such as KEEP= and DROP=, to tables. In the SQL procedure, SAS data set options (separated with spaces) are enclosed with parentheses and follow immediately after the table name. Thus the template for one form of the CREATE TABLE statement is

CREATE TABLE <*libref.*>*table* <(*dataset-option* <*dataset-option*>...)>

You can also use SAS data set options on tables or SAS/ACCESS views listed in the FROM clause of a query. See "Creating Tables with the SQL Procedure" later in this chapter for a full description of the CREATE TABLE statement.

You cannot associate SAS data set options with PROC SQL view names as they are only valid for a view's underlying tables. For example, when you create a PROC SQL view, you cannot list SAS data set options after the view name. However, you can list data set options after the table name(s) in a view's FROM clause, provided those tables are not based on other PROC SQL views. See "Creating Views with the SQL Procedure" for more information on creating and using views.

When columns and their attributes are defined in a parenthesized list in the CREATE TABLE and CREATE INDEX statements, SAS data set options can be added to that list (without repeating the parentheses) as long as the options are separated from the columns by commas. See the first example for this type of use.

Examples

The first example creates a permanent table that is stored in the SAS data library pointed to by SQL; the SAS data set options TYPE= and LABEL= are specified. Here, the data set options are included in the parenthesized list defining the table's columns and attributes.

```
proc sql;
create table sql.salaries(type=data label='Salaries Table',
        lastname char(14),
        fname char(10),
        ssnumber num format=SSN11.,
        salary num label='Monthly Salary' format=dollar10.2,
        annsal num label='Annual Salary' format=dollar10.2);

insert into sql.salaries
    values('Conway','Kathryn',224223312,4325,51900)
    values('Schneyer','Samantha',321538796,1275,15300)
    values('Stein','Joel',323093467,3211,38532)
    values('Rodriguez','Jose',123994563,3356,40272)
    values('Johnston','Lois',276116745,2444,29328)
    values('Wong','William',321684532,1798,21576);

title 'Salaries Table';
select * from sql.salaries;
```

```
                              Salaries Table                            1

                                                Monthly    Annual
        LASTNAME       FNAME      SSNUMBER       Salary     Salary
        -------------------------------------------------------------
        Conway         Kathryn    224-22-3312    $4,325.00  $51,900.00
        Schneyer       Samantha   321-53-8796    $1,275.00  $15,300.00
        Stein          Joel       323-09-3467    $3,211.00  $38,532.00
        Rodriguez      Jose       123-99-4563    $3,356.00  $40,272.00
        Johnston       Lois       276-11-6745    $2,444.00  $29,328.00
        Wong           William    321-68-4532    $1,798.00  $21,576.00
```

If you run the CONTENTS procedure on this table, you will see the label assigned to it. (This procedure was run under the MVS/XA host system on an IBM computer; results may vary from system to system.)

```
proc contents data=sql.salaries;
run;
```

```
                                                                        1
                         CONTENTS PROCEDURE

   Data Set Name: SQL.SALARIES            Observations:         6
   Member Type:   DATA                    Variables:            5
   Engine:        V606                    Indexes:              0
   Created:       15DEC89:13:35:27        Observation Length:   48
   Last Modified: 15DEC89:13:35:28        Deleted Observations: 0
   Data Set Type: DATA                    Compressed:           NO
   Label:         Salaries Table

            -----Alphabetic List of Variables and Attributes-----

     #   Variable   Type   Len   Pos   Format      Label
    ----------------------------------------------------------------
     5   ANNSAL     Num     8    40    DOLLAR10.2  Annual Salary
     2   FNAME      Char   10    14
     1   LASTNAME   Char   14     0
     4   SALARY     Num     8    32    DOLLAR10.2  Monthly Salary
     3   SSNUMBER   Num     8    24    SSN11.

            -----Engine/Host Dependent Information-----

       Data Set Page Size:       6144
       Number of Data Set Pages: 1
       First Data Page:          1
       Max Obs per Page:         101
       Obs in First Data Page:   6
       Physical Name:            SAS-DATA-SET
       Release created:          6.06
       Release last modified:    6.06
       Created:                  13:35 FRIDAY, DECEMBER 15, 1989
       Created by:               SASUSER
       Last modified:            13:35 FRIDAY, DECEMBER 15, 1989
       Last modified by:         SASUSER
       Subextents:               1
       Total blocks used:        1
```

The second example creates another table using a different form of the CREATE TABLE statement. In this case, the LABEL= option is in a separate parenthesized list before the table definition.

```
create table sql.midrange(label='Midrange Salaries') as
   select *
      from sql.salaries
      where salary>2000 and salary<3999;

select * from sql.midrange;
```

```
                                                                        1
                                          Monthly    Annual
    LASTNAME      FNAME       SSNUMBER      Salary     Salary
    ---------------------------------------------------------------
    Stein         Joel       323-09-3467  $3,211.00  $38,532.00
    Rodriguez     Jose       123-99-4563  $3,356.00  $40,272.00
    Johnston      Lois       276-11-6745  $2,444.00  $29,328.00
```

This last example creates a temporarily stored PROC SQL view, Lowsals, based on the Salaries table. Notice that the DROP= data set option is listed on the view's underlying table.

```
create view lowsals as
   select *
      from sql.salaries(drop=annsal)
      where salary<2000;

select * from lowsals;
```

```
                                                      Monthly        1
              LASTNAME       FNAME       SSNUMBER      Salary
              --------------------------------------------------
              Schneyer       Samantha    321-53-8796   $1,275.00
              Wong           William     321-68-4532   $1,798.00
```

See *SAS Language: Reference* for a list of SAS data set options.

Statements in the SQL Procedure

The statements used in the SQL procedure are described in the following sections. Because the statements are presented in alphabetical order, some terms are referred to before they are defined. Use the book's index or the "See Also" section of each description to refer to other statement or component descriptions that may be helpful.

ALTER Statement

changes the attributes of columns or adds columns to or drops columns from a table.

Format

ALTER TABLE table-name
    <**ADD** column-definition <, column-definition>... >
    <**MODIFY** column-definition <, column-definition>... >
    <**DROP** column-name <, column-name>... >;

Description
The ALTER statement adds columns to or drops columns from an existing table. It is also used to change column attributes in an existing table. This statement cannot reference PROC SQL views or SAS/ACCESS views.

When the ALTER statement adds a column to the table, it initializes the column's values to missing in all rows of the table. You can then use the UPDATE statement to add values to the new column(s).

ALTER Statement *continued*

If a column is already in the table, you can change the following column (variable) attributes using the MODIFY clause: length, informat, format, and label. The values in a table are truncated or padded with blanks (if character data) as necessary to meet the specified length attribute. See "object-item" later in this chapter and *SAS Language: Reference* for more information on these variable attributes.

To change a column's name, you must use the RENAME= SAS data set option. You cannot change this attribute with the ALTER statement. You also cannot change a column's data type: that is, you cannot change a character column to numeric and vice versa.

If you want to drop a column and all its values from a table, specify the column's name in the DROP clause. If you modify or drop a column that is referenced in a view, the view's validity or meaning may be changed or damaged.

Altering an indexed column   When you alter the attributes of a column and an index has been defined for that column, the values in the altered column continue to have the index defined for them. In the example given in the next section, if the column CC has an index, the index still applies to the shortened values in the column.

If you drop a column with the ALTER statement, all the indexes (simple and composite) that the column participates in are also dropped. See the "CREATE Statement" later in this chapter for more information on creating and using indexes.

Examples

This example shows how you can use SAS code and the SQL procedure together. The DATA step creates Alterex, a permanent data set, and the SQL procedure alters its columns. The notes shown are written to the SAS log.

```
data sql.alterex;
   input cc $ nn;
   cards;
Hello 1
Goodbye 2
;

proc sql;
alter table sql.alterex
   modify cc  char(5),    /* this column will be shortened */
          nn2 num;        /* this column will be created   */

NOTE: The data set SQL.ALTEREX has 2 observations and 2 variables.
NOTE: Table SQL.ALTEREX modified, with 3 columns.
```

The new Alterex table is displayed as follows:

```
select * from sql.alterex;
```

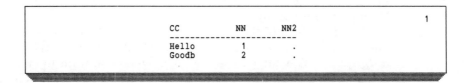

```
                                                                  1
                    CC        NN        NN2
                    ------------------------
                    Hello      1         .
                    Goodb      2         .
```

The following statement drops the NN2 column from the Alterex table. The note shown is written to the SAS log.

```
alter table sql.alterex
    drop nn2;
```

```
NOTE: Table SQL.ALTEREX modified, with 2 columns.
```

The modified Alterex table is displayed as follows:

```
select * from sql.alterex;
```

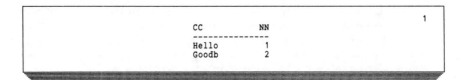

```
                                                                  1
                       CC        NN
                       ----------------
                       Hello      1
                       Goodb      2
```

See Also
column-definition, object-item, table-name ALTER statement

CREATE Statement

creates tables, views, and indexes on columns in tables.

The CREATE statement enables you to create tables, PROC SQL views that are based on tables or other views, and indexes on columns in tables. Each use is described in a separate section.

Creating Tables with the SQL Procedure

Format

CREATE TABLE table-name (column-definition <, column-definition>...);

CREATE TABLE table-name **AS** query-expression;

CREATE TABLE table-name **LIKE** table-name;

CREATE Statement *continued*

Description
The SQL procedure has three ways of creating tables (or SAS data files), each having certain advantages.

The first form of the CREATE TABLE statement (as listed in "Format") creates tables that automatically map SQL data types to those supported by the SAS System. You should use this form when you want to create a new table with columns that are not already present in existing tables. It is also useful if you are running SQL statements from an SQL application in another SQL-based database. (See "column-definition" later in this chapter for more information on data types in the SQL procedure.)

This form creates a new table without rows. You can then use an INSERT statement to add rows to the table or the ALTER statement to modify column attributes or to add or drop columns.

The second form of the CREATE TABLE statement (as listed in "Format") stores the results of any query-expression in a table, instead of displaying the query results in SAS output. That is, the data in the source table(s) are copied into the new table, as specified or modified by any expressions in the query-expression. It is a convenient way of setting up tables that are subsets or supersets of other tables, views, or SAS/ACCESS views.

Using this second form, you physically create a table as the statement is executed. If the underlying tables (in the query-expression) are changed after execution, the change(s) will not appear in the newly created table. If you want the change(s) reflected, you should create a view, which is evaluated each time it is referenced and therefore reflects the most current data and format in the underlying tables. See "Creating Views with the SQL Procedure" later in this section.

The third form of the CREATE TABLE statement (as listed in "Format") uses a LIKE clause to create a table that has the same column names and column attributes as another table. If you want to drop any columns in the new table, you can specify the DROP= SAS data set option with the new table name in the CREATE TABLE statement. The specified column(s) will be dropped when the table is created.

This form also creates a table without rows. You can use an INSERT statement to add rows or the ALTER statement to modify column attributes or to add or drop columns.

Librefs and storing tables   If you want to create a permanently stored table, you must specify the SAS data library (using a libref) in which the table will be stored. For example, for the two-level name SQL.EMPLOYEE, SQL is a libref pointing to the data library and EMPLOYEE is the name of the table. If you create a temporarily stored table, you may omit the libref; in this case, the default temporary library, WORK, is assumed. See "table-name" later in this chapter for more information on librefs and storing tables.

Example

This example uses the SQL procedure to create the temporary table Service and uses the SAS PRINT procedure to display it.

```
proc sql;
create table service as
   select empname, empyears
      from sql.employee
      where empboss is not null;

proc print noobs;
   title 'Employee Service Records';
run;
```

```
                    Employee Service Records                    1

                       EMPNAME    EMPYEARS

                       Betty          8
                       Joe            2
                       Jeff           1
                       Wanda         10
                       Fred           6
                       Sally          9
                       Marvin         5
                       Nick           1
                       Chuck         12
                       Sam            7
```

You could also use a query-expression to display this same output table:

```
proc sql;
select * from service;
```

See also "Creating a Table" in Chapter 3 for other examples.

Creating Views with the SQL Procedure

Format

> **CREATE VIEW** *view-name* **AS** query-expression
> <**ORDER BY** order-by-item <, order-by-item>... >;

Description

A PROC SQL view is a query-expression that is given a name and stored for later use. Some host systems only allow names to be up to seven characters long, unlike SAS System names which can be up to eight characters. For this reason, the view names used in this book are no longer than seven characters.

You can refer to views in queries as if they were tables, but a view is not the same as a table. A table is stored data while a view is a stored query-expression, that is, a description or definition of a virtual table. When you define a view and submit it, the view derives its data from the tables, views, or SAS/ACCESS views listed in its FROM clause. The data accessed by a view are a subset or superset of the data in its underlying table(s) or of the data derived from its underlying PROC SQL or SAS/ACCESS view(s).

CREATE Statement *continued*

When a view is referenced by another PROC SQL statement, by a SAS procedure, or in a DATA step, it is executed and, conceptually, an internal table is built by the SQL procedure. The SQL procedure then processes this internal table as if it were any table. For example, a view's columns can be renamed with aliases or labels; summary functions and arithmetic calculations can be performed on a column's values; or a view's columns can be joined with columns in other tables, views, or SAS/ACCESS views.

Because a PROC SQL view is a stored query-expression and contains no data, you cannot update it as you would a table. A PROC SQL view is a read-only object. In Release 6.06 of the SAS System, you cannot use a view to update the data in that view's underlying tables. That is, you cannot use the INSERT, DELETE, UPDATE, or ALTER statements when referencing a PROC SQL view. You cannot update the data accessed by a PROC SQL view using a SAS procedure such as FSEDIT.

You can use the SQL procedure to update the DBMS data described by a SAS/ACCESS view if the SAS/ACCESS view is created so that it can be updated. See "DELETE Statement," "INSERT Statement," and "UPDATE Statement" later in this chapter for more information.

Unlike many SQL databases, the SQL procedure allows you to specify the ORDER BY clause in the CREATE VIEW statement. Each time a view is referenced and processed, its data are sorted and displayed as specified by the ORDER BY clause. This sorting on every access has certain performance costs, especially if the view's underlying tables are large. You may want to omit the ORDER BY clause when creating the view and specify it on an as-needed basis when referencing the view in queries.

When you reference a PROC SQL (or SAS/ACCESS view) using the SQL procedure, DATA step, or other SAS procedure, the view is evaluated against the current state of the underlying data. Therefore, accessing data through a view gives you the most up-to-date information. Storing a subset of a table, for example, is current only at the time the data are stored—the data may be out-of-date by the time you use them.

Librefs and stored views   Storing tables using first-level names (librefs) and second-level names (table names) is described earlier in this chapter in "Creating Tables with the SQL Procedure." Using a second-level name alone in the SAS System usually indicates a temporarily stored table, except in the case of PROC SQL views. You can refer to a table name alone (without the libref) in the FROM clause of a CREATE VIEW statement if the table and view reside in the same data library, as in this example:

```
proc sql;
create view sql.view1 as
   select * from invoice where invqty>10;
```

In this view definition, View1 and Invoice are stored permanently in the same data library pointed to by SQL. Specifying a libref for Invoice is optional and gives you some degree of independence in using different librefs for the same library. If the libref were required in the FROM clause, you would always have to have associated the data library to that libref when using the view.

If the view and the table will reside in different SAS data libraries, you must specify a libref with the table name when you create the view.

Examples

Data often need transforming before they can be used. A good example is the storing of a person's age. It is better to store someone's birthday so that the data will not be out of date when you use them next year, but you would rather see the data in terms of years old when you use the table. This example creates the Birthday data set and then uses the SQL procedure to create and display a view derived from the data set. The notes shown are written to the log.

```
data sql.birthday;
   input name $ bday date7.;
   format bday date7.;
   cards;
Jenny 04feb63
Sally 10feb66
;

proc sql;
create view sql.bday as
   select name, bday,
          (today()-bday)/365.25 as age format=6.2
       from birthday
       order by name;
```

```
NOTE:  The data set SQL.BIRTHDAY has 2 observations and 3 variables.
NOTE:  SQL view SQL.BDAY has been defined.
```

Notice that only the second-level name is used in this view because the permanent table it refers to is in the same SAS data library as the view itself.

When a column alias is used in a view definition, as AGE is used in the previous example, the alias becomes the permanent name of the column for each execution of the view. Likewise, the format defined for this column becomes the permanent, default output format.

The SAS log displays a message that the view has been defined, so you can perform a query on the new view and see the following output:

```
title 'Data Set with Ages Computed';
select * from sql.bday;
```

```
                    Data Set with Ages Computed                    1

             NAME          BDAY      AGE
             -------------------------------
             Jenny       04FEB63    26.48
             Sally       10FEB66    23.46
```

CREATE Statement *continued*

This next example shows that a view can also be used in SAS procedures other than the SQL procedure.

```
proc print data=sql.bday;
   title 'Views Can Be Accessed by Other SAS Procedures';
run;
```

```
          Views Can Be Accessed by Other SAS Procedures          1

               OBS     NAME      BDAY      AGE

                1      Jenny     04FEB63    26.48
                2      Sally     10FEB66    23.46
```

Notice that if you run this example, the AGE results will be different than those in the example because AGE is calculated with the SAS function TODAY().

Creating Indexes with the SQL Procedure

Format

CREATE < **UNIQUE** > **INDEX** *index-name*
   ON table-name (column-name <, column-name>...);

Description
An index stores the values of a table's columns and a system of directions that enable the SAS System, under certain circumstances, to locate rows in a table more quickly and efficiently. In particular, indexes enable the SQL procedure to process certain classes of queries more efficiently:

□ comparisons against a column that is indexed

□ IN subquery where the column in the inner subquery is indexed

□ correlated subqueries, where the column being compared with the correlated reference is indexed

□ join-queries, where the join condition is an equals comparison and all the columns involved in the join-expression are indexed in one of the tables being joined.

The SAS System determines the most efficient way to process a query or statement, and therefore, it determines whether or not to use an index in processing. You cannot tell the SAS System to use an index that you have defined on a column or set of columns.

Indexes are maintained by the SAS System for all changes to the table, whether the changes originate from the SQL procedure or some other source. That is, even if you alter a column's definition or update its values, the same index continues to be defined for it.

You can create simple or composite indexes. A *simple index* is created on one column in a table. The default V606 engine requires a simple index to have the same name as that column, as shown in the first example in "Examples." See *SAS Language: Reference* for more information on the V606 engine.

A *composite index* is one index name that is defined for two or more columns, as shown in the second example in "Examples." The columns can be specified in any order, and they can have different data types. A composite index name cannot match the name of one of its columns. If you drop a composite index, the index is dropped for all the columns named in that composite index.

Indexes are used to make queries retrieve and evaluate data more efficiently. Using a composite index to identify and group columns can further speed this process. For example, in a large personnel table, you would want to have a composite index NAME over the columns FRSTNAME and LASTNAME. This combination enables a query to find an employee's name faster than if a simple index were defined for just one of these columns.

You should be careful not to define more than one composite index for the same set of columns. That is, do not create one composite index called NAMES on the columns FRSTNAME and LASTNAME and later define another index for the same columns (in the same order) but call it BOTHNAME. You will get an error message in the SAS log if you try to do this. When in doubt, display the table definition with the CONTENTS procedure to see the index names and the columns for which they are defined.

The UNIQUE keyword causes the SAS System to reject any change to a table that would cause more than one row to have the same data value (and therefore, same index value). Unique indexes guarantee that data in one column, or a composite group of columns, remain unique for every value in a table. For this reason, a unique index should not be defined for a column that could include NULL or missing values. In a personnel table, for example, each employee's social security number should be unique, so you can create a unique index over that column.

For more information on using indexes to improve performance, see the "Role of Indexes in Equijoins" and "Improving Query Performance" in Chapter 4, "Using the Advanced Features of the SQL Procedure." Creating and deleting indexes are described briefly in Chapter 17, "The DATASETS Procedure," in the *SAS Procedures Guide*. A lengthy description of indexes, when to specify them, and how they affect other SAS statements is included in Chapter 6, "SAS Files," in *SAS Language: Reference*.

Examples

This example creates a simple index on the EMPNUM column of the Employee table. The note is written to the SAS log.

```
proc sql;
create unique index empnum on sql.employee(empnum);

NOTE:  Simple index EMPNUM has been defined.
```

If you specify the UNIQUE keyword and try to insert a row that includes the same employee number (EMPNUM) as a current employee, you will receive an error message, the row will not be inserted, and the table will remain unchanged.

CREATE Statement *continued*

In the next example, a composite index is defined on two columns to identify a customer. The note is written to the SAS log.

```
create index custno on sql.customer (custname, custnum);

NOTE:  Composite index CUSTNO has been defined.
```

See Also
column-definition, column-name, query-expression, table-name

DELETE Statement

removes rows from a table, as specified in the WHERE expression.

Format

DELETE
    FROM table-name | *<libref.>sas-access-view* **<AS** *alias>*
    <WHERE sql-expression>;

Description
This statement removes all the rows from the table or SAS/ACCESS view specified in the FROM clause, for which the WHERE expression is true. This statement cannot reference PROC SQL views in its FROM clause.

▶ *Caution* . . . . *If the WHERE clause is not specified, the DELETE statement deletes all the rows from the table or SAS/ACCESS view.* ▲

Using SAS/ACCESS views in the DELETE statement   You can refer to a SAS/ACCESS view (or view descriptor) in the FROM clause of a DELETE statement in the following cases:

☐ You have been granted the appropriate authorization by the external database management system (for example, DB2) to delete rows from a table.

☐ The SAS/ACCESS view describes data from an external database table (such as a DB2 table). The DELETE statement removes rows from the external database table.

☐ The SAS/ACCESS view describes data from an external database view (such as a DB2 view) that is based on a single database table. The DELETE statement removes rows from the single database table.

    You cannot use the DELETE statement when referencing a SAS/ACCESS view that describes data from an external database view that is based on multiple database tables or database views.

See the SAS/ACCESS interface guide for your database system for more information.

Example

In this example, a copy is made of the Customer table so that the permanently stored table is not modified. All the customers with stores in Virginia Beach are then eliminated. The notes shown are written to the SAS log.

```
proc sql;
create table cities as
   select * from sql.customer;

delete
   from cities
   where custcity='Virginia Beach';

select * from cities;

NOTE:  Table WORK.CITIES created, with 16 rows and 3 columns.
NOTE:  3 rows were deleted from WORK.CITIES.
```

```
                                                                       1
     CUSTNAME     CUSTNUM  CUSTCITY
     --------------------------------------------
     Beach Land        16  Ocean City
     Coast Shop         3  Myrtle Beach
     Coast Shop         5  Myrtle Beach
     Coast Shop        14  Charleston
     Del Mar            3  Folly Beach
     Del Mar            8  Charleston
     Del Mar           11  Charleston
     New Waves          3  Ocean City
     Sea Sports         8  Charleston
     Surf Mart        101  Charleston
     Surf Mart        118  Surfside
     Surf Mart        127  Ocean Isle
     Surf Mart        133  Charleston
```

See Also

sql-expression, table-name

DESCRIBE Statement

displays a view definition in the SAS log.

Format

DESCRIBE VIEW *view-name*;

Description

The DESCRIBE statement displays the definition of a PROC SQL view in the SAS log. This statement is helpful for reminding the user how the view is defined.

This statement can only be specified for PROC SQL views. To get more information on a table or SAS/ACCESS view, use the PROC SQL statement's FEEDBACK option described earlier in this chapter.

DESCRIBE Statement *continued*

Example
This example creates the Manager view.

```
proc sql;
create view sql.manager as
   select empnum, empname, empcity
      from sql.employee
      where emptitle='manager';

title 'Managers';
select * from sql.manager;
```

```
                             Managers                              1

              EMPNUM  EMPNAME   EMPCITY
              -------------------------------------
                 201  Betty     Ocean City
                 301  Sally     Wilmington
                 401  Chuck     Charleston
```

If you then specify the DESCRIBE statement as follows, a message appears in the SAS log:

```
describe view sql.manager;
```

```
SAS LOG

COMMAND ===>

NOTE:  SQL view SQL.MANAGER is defined as:

     select EMPNUM, EMPNAME, EMPCITY
       from SQL.EMPLOYEE
       where EMPTITLE='manager';
```

See Also
CREATE statement

DROP Statement

deletes the specified table, view, or index.

Format

DROP TABLE table-name <, table-name>... ;
DROP VIEW *view-name* <, *view-name*>... ;
DROP INDEX *index-name* <, *index-name*>... **FROM** table-name;

Description

The DROP statement deletes the entire table, PROC SQL view, or index requested. If a table or view has been stored permanently, you must qualify the name with its libref. If you drop a table that is referenced in a PROC SQL view definition and try to execute the view, an error message is displayed stating that the table does not exist. Therefore, remove references in queries to any table(s) and view(s) that you drop.

If you drop a table with indexed columns, all the indexes are automatically dropped. If you drop a composite index, the index is dropped for all the columns named in that index.

You cannot use the DROP statement to drop a table or view in an external database that is described by a SAS/ACCESS view.

Examples

This example creates the Salereps table and the index EMPNUM and produces notes in the SAS log. The DROP statements drop the specified index and table, respectively.

```
proc sql;
create table sql.salereps as
   select empnum
      from sql.employee
      where emptitle='salesrep';

create index empnum on sql.salereps (empnum);

NOTE:  Table SQL.SALEREPS created, with 7 rows and 1 column.
NOTE:  Simple index EMPNUM has been defined.

drop index empnum from sql.salereps;

NOTE: Index EMPNUM has been dropped.

drop table sql.salereps;

NOTE: Table SQL.SALEREPS has been dropped.
```

DROP Statement *continued*

In "Creating Indexes with the SQL Procedure" earlier in this chapter, a composite index CUSTNO was defined for the CUSTNAME and CUSTNUM columns. The DROP statement is used here to drop this composite index.

```
drop index custno from sql.customer;

NOTE: Index CUSTNAME has been dropped.
NOTE: Index CUSTNUM has been dropped.
```

See Also
CREATE statement, table-name

INSERT Statement

inserts a new row into a table.

Format

INSERT INTO table-name | <*libref.*>*sas-access-view*
      <(column-name <, column-name>...)>
   set-clause <set-clause>... ;

INSERT INTO table-name | <*libref.*>*sas-access-view*
      <(column-name <, column-name>...)>
   values-clause <values-clause>... ;

INSERT INTO table-name | <*libref.*>*sas-access-view*
      <(column-name <, column-name>...)>
   query-expression;

Description
The INSERT statement adds new rows to a new or existing table, setting the values of the columns in one of three ways. This statement can only be used with tables and SAS/ACCESS views, not PROC SQL views.* If the INSERT statement includes an optional list of column names, only those columns will be given values by the statement; columns that are in the table but not listed are given missing values.

The first form of the INSERT statement (as listed in "Format") uses the SET clause, which sets or alters the values of a column. You can use more than one SET clause per INSERT statement, and each SET clause can set more than one column. If you specify an optional list of columns, you can only set a value for a column that is specified in the list of columns to be inserted. See "set-clause" later in this chapter for more information.

---

*   For simplicity, *table* is used in the rest of the description to mean *table* or *SAS/ACCESS view.*

The second form of the INSERT statement (as listed in "Format") uses the VALUES clause. This clause can be used to insert lists of values into a table. You can either give a value for each column in the table or give values just for the columns specified in the list of column names. One row is inserted for each VALUES clause. The order of the values in the VALUES clause matches the order of the column names in the INSERT column list or, if no list was specified, the order of the columns in the table. See "values-clause" later in this chapter for more information.

The third form of the INSERT statement (as listed in "Format") inserts the results of a query-expression into a table. The order of the values in the query-expression matches the order of the column names in the INSERT column list or, if no list was specified, the order of the columns in the table. See "query-expression" later in this chapter for more information.

Using SAS/ACCESS views in the INSERT statement   You can refer to a SAS/ACCESS view (or view descriptor) in the INTO clause of an INSERT statement in the following cases:

□   You have been granted the appropriate authorization by the external database management system (for example, DB2) to insert rows into a table.

□   The SAS/ACCESS view describes data from an external database table (such as a DB2 table). The INSERT statement adds rows to the external database table.

□   The SAS/ACCESS view describes data from an external database view (such as a DB2 view) that is based on a single database table. The INSERT statement adds rows to the single database table.

    You cannot use the INSERT statement when referencing a SAS/ACCESS view that describes data from an external database view that is based on multiple database tables or database views.

See the SAS/ACCESS interface guide for your database system for more information.

Inserting a row when a column is indexed   Because an index is defined on a column, if you insert a new row into a table, that value will be added to the index. Suppose, for example, that you add a new row to the Employee table and the column EMPNUM has a simple index defined on it:

```
proc sql;
insert into sql.employee
   values(420,'Susan',1,'Charleston','salesrep',401);

select * from sql.employee;
```

INSERT Statement *continued*

```
                                                                          1
   EMPNUM  EMPNAME  EMPYEARS  EMPCITY           EMPTITLE   EMPBOSS
   ---------------------------------------------------------------------
      101  Herb          28  Ocean City        president      .
      201  Betty          8  Ocean City        manager      101
      213  Joe            2  Virginia Beach    salesrep     201
      214  Jeff           1  Virginia Beach    salesrep     201
      215  Wanda         10  Ocean City        salesrep     201
      216  Fred           6  Ocean City        salesrep     201
      301  Sally          9  Wilmington        manager      101
      314  Marvin         5  Wilmington        salesrep     301
      318  Nick           1  Myrtle Beach      salesrep     301
      401  Chuck         12  Charleston        manager      101
      417  Sam            7  Charleston        salesrep     401
      420  Susan          1  Charleston        salesrep     401
```

The EMPNUM for **Susan**, 420, will also be indexed. (You can display a table's definition using the CONTENTS procedure; index names and the columns for which they are defined are also listed.) See "CREATE Statement" earlier in this chapter for more information on creating and using indexes.

Examples
The first example uses multiple SET clauses, where each SET clause has more than one column. Notice that the SET clauses are not separated by commas and the SET keyword is repeated for each row.

```
proc sql;
create table sql.insertex (x numeric, y numeric, z char);

insert into sql.insertex
   set x=1, y=3
   set z='hello', y=2
   set z='goodbye'
   ;

select * from sql.insertex;
```

```
                                              1
            X       Y   Z
            ----------------------------
            1       3
            .       2   hello
            .       .   goodbye
```

If you specify an optional list of columns after the table name, you can only specify those values in the SET clause. Thus, the following INSERT statement is rejected, as indicated by the message in the log, because Y is not listed with SQL.INSERTEX(X,Z).

```
insert into sql.insertex(x,z)
   set x=1, y=3
   ;
```

ERROR: Column Y is not on the list of columns to be inserted.

If you leave off the optional list of columns on the table name, the INSERT statement is valid, as shown in this example:

```
insert into sql.insertex
   set x=1, y=3
   ;
```

In the next example, the DELETE statement erases all the rows from the table before the VALUES clause is used to insert new rows and values for the columns. Deleting the rows is optional here; you can just insert the new rows into the table with the existing ones.

The VALUES clause adds rows to the empty Insertex table and then adds two more rows that contain missing values. Notice in this example that the VALUES clauses are not separated by commas and the VALUES keyword is repeated for each row.

```
delete from sql.insertex;

insert into sql.insertex
   values(1,2,'happy')
   values(3,4,'sad');

select * from sql.insertex;
```

```
                                                              1
                    X        Y   Z
            --------------------------
                    1        2   happy
                    3        4   sad
```

```
insert into sql.insertex(z,y)
   values('happier',5)
   values('very sad',6);

select * from sql.insertex;
```

INSERT Statement *continued*

```
                                                                     1
                    X       Y  Z
        -----------------------------
                    1       2  happy
                    3       4  sad
                    .       5  happier
                    .       6  very sad
```

In the following example, the results of a query are inserted into a table. Notice that the order of the values in the query-expression matches the order of the columns in the INSERT column list.

```
delete from sql.insertex;

insert into sql.insertex(z,x,y)
   select empname, empnum, empyears
      from sql.employee
      where empname like 'J%';

select * from sql.insertex;
```

```
                                                                     1
                    X       Y  Z
        -----------------------------
                  213       2  Joe
                  214       1  Jeff
```

See Also
column-name, query-expression, set-clause, table-name, values-clause

---

SELECT Statement

retrieves data for the query, formats the selected rows, and prints it in SAS output.

Format

query-expression
    <**ORDER BY** order-by-item <, order-by-item>... >;

Description
The SELECT statement evaluates the query, formats the rows selected into a report, and prints (displays) it in SAS output. The SELECT statement provides the *query* in the Structured Query Language.

The SELECT statement is included in the query-expression. A *query-expression* may be a simple table-expression (as described in the next paragraph) or a combination of more than one table-expression. Think of each table-expression as producing a set of data, which you can combine with the SQL set operators UNION, INTERSECT, EXCEPT, and OUTER UNION.

A *table-expression* is composed of the SELECT and FROM clauses, as well as other optional clauses, as shown here.

SELECT <**DISTINCT**> object-item(s)	SELECT clause
<**INTO** host-variable(s)>	INTO clause
FROM from-list	FROM clause
<where-expression>	WHERE clause
<**GROUP BY** group-by-item(s)>	GROUP BY clause
<having-expression>	HAVING clause

Most query-expressions do not involve set operators and are just a single table-expressions terminated with a semicolon. See "table-expression" and "query-expression" later in this chapter for more information; set operators and how they are used is described in "query-expression."

If the NOPRINT option has been specified in the PROC SQL statement, no result table is displayed in SAS output. If an INTO clause is specified in a table-expression while the NOPRINT option is in effect, the query still executes so that the macro variables specified in that clause can be set.

The SELECT statement can also be used to retrieve data from an external database management system by means of the SAS/ACCESS software. You can use this software to create SAS/ACCESS views (or view descriptors) that describe data from a DB2 table, for example, to the SAS System. You can use SAS/ACCESS views as you would PROC SQL tables, with some restrictions, as noted in the INSERT, DELETE, and UPDATE statement descriptions elsewhere in this chapter. See the SAS/ACCESS interface guide to your external database system for more information on using SAS/ACCESS views.

Example

Examples of the SELECT statement are used throughout this book; examples with the set operators are included in Chapter 3 and in "query-expression" later in this chapter. This example shows a typical SELECT statement; the note is written to the SAS log.

```
proc sql;
select empname                    /* lists all employees */
   from sql.employee              /* in seniority order   */
   order by empyears desc;

NOTE: The query as specified involves ordering by an item that doesn't
      appear in its SELECT clause.
```

SELECT Statement *continued*

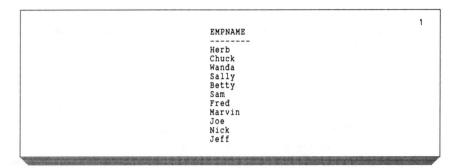

See Also

host-variable, query-expression, table-name, table-expression

---

UPDATE Statement

modifies the values of columns in existing rows of a table.

Format

UPDATE table-name | *<libref.>sas-access-view* **<AS** *alias>*
   set-clause
   <where-expression>;

Description

The UPDATE statement modifies the values in a column in existing rows of a table or SAS/ACCESS view according to the values specified in the SET clause;* see "set-clause" later in this chapter for more information on this component. (The UPDATE statement cannot reference a PROC SQL view as the table-name to be updated.) Any column that is not modified retains its original values, except in certain queries using the case-expression, as shown in "Examples" later in this section.

In the SET clause, a column reference on the left side of the equals sign can also appear as part of the sql-expression on the right side of the sign. That is, it is possible to modify a column in terms of itself, for example, to give the sales representatives a $1000 holiday bonus:

```
set salary=salary+1000
```

All the rows specified by the WHERE expression are updated. If you omit the WHERE expression, all the rows in the table are updated.

---

* For simplicity, *table* is used in the rest of this description to mean *table* or *SAS/ACCESS view.*

Using SAS/ACCESS views in the UPDATE statement   You can reference a SAS/ACCESS view (or view descriptor) in the UPDATE statement in the following cases:

□   You have been granted the appropriate authorization by the external database management system (for example, DB2) to update data in a table.

□   The SAS/ACCESS view describes data from an external database table (such as a DB2 table). The UPDATE statement modifies the data in the external database table.

□   The SAS/ACCESS view describes data from an external database view (such as a DB2 view) that is based on a single database table. The UPDATE statement modifies the data in the single database table.

     You cannot use the UPDATE statement when referencing a SAS/ACCESS view that describes data from an external database view that is based on multiple database tables or database views.

     See the SAS/ACCESS interface guide for your database system for more information.

Updating an indexed column   When you update a column and an index has been defined for that column, the values in the updated column continue to have the index defined for them. In the first example in the following section, if PRODLIST has an index, the old values of PRODLIST are removed from the index and replaced with the newly increased values in this column.

Examples

A temporary table has been created in this example to avoid changing the permanently stored table. In practice, you can update the permanent table directly.

     In this example, management has decided to increase the list price of items less than $1000 by 10% and more expensive items by 20%, except for kayaks. The first UPDATE statement uses a CASE expression to select the multiplier, which updates the data in one pass. The notes are written to the SAS log.

```
proc sql;
create table sql.updateex as
   select *, prodlist as oldlist
      from sql.product;

update sql.updateex
   set prodlist=prodlist*case when prodcost<1000 then 1.1
                             else 1.2
                             end
   where prodname not='kayak';

select * from sql.updateex;

NOTE:  Table SQL.UPDATEEX created, with 7 rows and 3 columns.
NOTE:  6 rows were updated in SQL.UPDATEEX.
```

UPDATE Statement *continued*

```
                                                                    1
          PRODNAME   PRODCOST  PRODLIST  OLDLIST
          -----------------------------------------
          flippers       $16       $22      $20
          jet ski     $2,150    $3,210   $2,675
          kayak         $190      $240     $240
          raft            $5        $8       $7
          snorkel        $12       $17      $15
          surfboard     $615      $825     $750
          windsurfer  $1,090    $1,590   $1,325
```

Notice that if this query had no ELSE expression, the result of the case-expression would be a missing value for any row processed that did not meet the WHEN condition criteria. If no WHERE expression is specified, all the rows in the Updateex table are processed.

Two UPDATE statements with WHERE expressions that specify the appropriate ranges can produce the same effect.

```
update sql.updateex
   set prodlist=prodlist*1.1
   where prodname not='kayak' and prodcost<1000;

update sql.updateex
   set prodlist=prodlist*1.2
   where prodname not='kayak' and prodcost>=1000;
```

If you do not use a case-expression, you must use two UPDATE statements to modify the Updateex data.

Evaluating multiple UPDATE statements   The ANSI Standard for SQL requires that expressions in the SET clause be evaluated before updating any row in the table. Take the following table for example:

```
proc sql;
create table numbers (a int,b int);
insert into numbers values(1,10) values(2,20);

title 'Numbers Table';
select * from numbers;

update numbers
   set a=a+5, b=b+a;

title 'Updated Numbers Table';
select * from numbers;
```

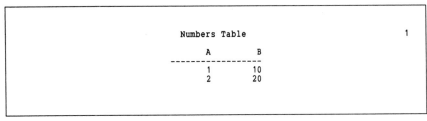

Notice in the output of the Updated Numbers Table that the original value of A is used to calculate B+A; *the updated value of A is not used*. To use the updated value of A, you must write two queries.

See Also
case-expression, set-clause, table-name, where-expression

VALIDATE Statement

checks a query-expression for syntactic accuracy.

Format

VALIDATE query-expression;

Description
This statement checks the correctness of a query-expression's syntax without executing the expression. If valid, a message to that effect is displayed in the SAS log; if invalid, an error message is displayed.

The VALIDATE statement can also be included in applications that use the macro facility. When used in such an application, the VALIDATE statement returns a value indicating the query-expression's validity. The value is returned through the macro variable SQLRC (short for SQL return code). For example, if a SELECT statement is valid, the macro variable SQLRC returns a value less than or equal to 4. See "Macro Variables Set by Statements in the SQL Procedure," for more information on these values.

The VALIDATE statement is useful in interactive applications for determining whether a PROC SQL query is likely to succeed if actually submitted.

VALIDATE Statement *continued*

Example
This example checks the query for syntactic accuracy and writes a message in
the SAS log.

```
proc sql;
validate
   select custname, custcity
      from sql.customer
      where custcity contains 'Beach';

NOTE: PROC SQL statement has valid syntax.
```

A SAS/AF software application enables a user to type in a SELECT statement
that defines a view.* Before issuing the CREATE VIEW statement, the
application checks to see if the view will be accessible.

```
submit sql continue;
   validate &viewdef;
endsubmit;

if symget('SQLRC')>4 then
   do;
      ... the view is not valid ...
   end;
else do;
   submit sql continue;
      create view &viewname as &viewdef;
   endsubmit;
end;
```

See Also
table-expression

Macro Variables Set by Statements in the SQL Procedure

The SQL procedure sets up automatic macro variables with certain values after
it executes each statement. These macro variables can be tested inside a macro to
determine whether to continue processing. SAS/AF software users can also test
them from a Screen Control Language (SCL) program after a **SUBMIT SQL;** block
of code (using the SYMGET function).

---

*   See "Using This Book" for information on SAS/AF software documentation.

After each PROC SQL statement has executed, the following macro variables are updated with these values:

SQLOBS   contains the number of rows processed by an SQL procedure statement. For example, the number of rows formatted and displayed in SAS output by a SELECT statement or the number of rows deleted by a DELETE statement.

SQLRC   contains a status value indicating the success of the SQL procedure statement.

> 0 PROC SQL statement completed successfully with no errors.
>
> 4 PROC SQL statement encountered a situation for which it issues a warning. The statement continued to execute.
>
> 8 PROC SQL statement encountered an error. The statement stops execution at this point.
>
> 12 PROC SQL statement encountered an internal error, indicating a bug in the SQL procedure that should be reported to SAS Institute.
>
> These errors can only occur during compile time.
>
> 16 PROC SQL statement encountered a user error. This error code is used, for example, when a subquery (that can only return a single value) evaluates to more than one row. These errors can only be detected during run time.
>
> 24 PROC SQL statement encountered a systems error. This error is used, for example, if the system cannot write to a SAS data set because the disk is full. These errors can only occur during run time.
>
> 28 PROC SQL statement encountered an internal error, indicating a bug in the SQL procedure that should be reported to SAS Institute. These errors can only occur during run time.

SQLOOPS   contains the number of iterations that the inner loop of PROC SQL processes. The number of iterations increases proportionally with the complexity of the query. See also the LOOPS option in the PROC SQL statement.

This example retrieves the data in the Employee table but does not display them in SAS output because of the NOPRINT option in the PROC SQL statement. The %PUT macro language statement is used to request and display the &SQL variable values.

```
proc sql noprint;
select * from sql.employee;
%put sqlobs=**&sqlobs**  sqloops=**&sqloops**  sqlrc=**&sqlrc**;
```

The following message is displayed in the SAS log, giving you the macro's values. Executing the PROC SQL statement replaces the &SQL variables with their current values.

```
SAS LOG

COMMAND ===>
...
1      proc sql noprint;
2      select * from sql.employee;
3      %put sqlobs=**&sqlobs** sqloops=**&sqloops** sqlrc=**&sqlrc**;
sqlobs=**1** sqloops=**11** sqlrc=**0**
```

Components of the SQL Procedure Statements

The components used in SQL procedure statements are described in the following sections. Because the components are presented in alphabetical order, some terms are referred to before they are defined. Use the book's index or the "See Also" section of each description to refer to other statement or component descriptions that may be helpful.

between-condition

searches for data lying within specified parameters.

Format

sql-expression <NOT> **BETWEEN** sql-expression **AND** sql-expression

Description

A BETWEEN condition selects rows where column values are within a range of values. The sql-expressions must be of compatible data types: that is, they must all be numeric or all character types. Because a BETWEEN condition evaluates the boundary values as a range, it is not necessary to specify the smaller quantity first.

You can use the NOT logical operator to exclude a range of numbers, for example, to eliminate customer numbers between 1 and 15 (inclusive) so that you can retrieve data on more recently acquired customers.

A BETWEEN condition is often used as a quick way to request data that lie inside a specific interval. Note that the SQL procedure also supports multiple comparison operators for compatibilty with the DATA step.

Examples

The following sql-expressions are all equivalent:

```
x between 1 and 3
x between 3 and 1
1<=x<=3
x>=1 and x<=3
```

This example lists invoices in which at least 10 but not more than 20 items have been sold:

```
proc sql;
select *
   from sql.invoice
   where invqty between 10 and 20;
```

```
                                                                         1
  INVNUM  CUSTNAME   CUSTNUM   EMPNUM  PRODNAME   INVQTY  INVPRICE
  --------------------------------------------------------------------
     280  Beach Land      16      215  snorkel        20      $14
     290  Beach Land      16      216  flippers       15      $19
     300  Beach Land      16      216  raft           20       $7
     340  Coast Shop       5      318  flippers       15      $19
     360  Coast Shop       5      318  snorkel        10      $15
     370  Coast Shop      12      213  raft           10       $7
     420  Del Mar         11      417  raft           15       $7
     430  Del Mar         11      417  snorkel        10      $15
     440  Del Mar         11      417  flippers       20      $19
     460  New Waves        3      215  flippers       10      $20
     470  New Waves        6      213  snorkel        15      $15
     490  New Waves        6      213  snorkel        10      $15
     500  Surf Mart      101      417  snorkel        20      $14
     520  Surf Mart      101      417  snorkel        12      $15
     530  Surf Mart      118      318  flippers       15      $19
     550  Surf Mart      118      318  snorkel        10      $15
```

See Also

sql-expression

case-expression

selects result values that satisfy specified conditions.

Format

CASE <*case-operand*>
　　WHEN *when-condition* **THEN** *result-expression*
　　<**WHEN** *when-condition* **THEN** *result-expression*>...
　　<**ELSE** *result-expression*>
　　END

Description

The CASE expression is used to select result values if certain conditions are met. A CASE expression returns a single value that is conditionally evaluated for each row of a table (or view). Use the WHEN-THEN clauses when you want to execute a CASE expression for some but not all of the rows in the table being queried or created. An optional ELSE expression gives an alternative action if any THEN expression is not executed.

The *case-operand*, *when-condition*, and *result-expression* must be valid sql-expressions. When *case-operand* is not specified, *when-condition* is evaluated as a Boolean value. When *when-condition* returns a nonzero, nonmissing result, the WHEN clause is true.

When *case-operand* is specified, it is compared with *when-condition* for equality. If *case-operand* equals *when-condition*, the WHEN clause is true.

The CASE expression is evaluated as follows. Depending on whether *case-operand* is specified (described earlier), *when-condition* is evaluated. If the *when-condition* is true for the row being processed, the *result-expression* following THEN is executed. If *when-condition* is false, SQL proceeds to the next *when-condition* until they are all evaluated. If every *when-condition* is false, SQL executes the ELSE expression and its result becomes the CASE expression's result. If no ELSE expression is present and every *when-condition* is false, the result of the CASE expression is a missing value.

Examples

The following example specifies *case-operand* in the first instance but not in the second. You can recode the numeric column Q1 so that 1 is yes, 2 is no, and anything else is no answer in these two ways. Remember, a CASE expression returns a single value (yes, no, or no answer) for each row it evaluates in the table.

```
case q1
   when 1 then 'yes'
   when 2 then 'no'
   else 'no answer'
   end

case
   when q1=1 then 'yes'
   when q1=2 then 'no'
   else 'no answer'
   end
```

In the next example, the form without a case-operand is necessary when *when-condition* does not involve equality tests.

```
proc sql;
select prodname,
       case
           when prodcost<50 then 'cheap'
           when prodcost<500 then 'not-so-cheap'
           when prodcost<1000 then 'expensive'
           else 'outrageous'
       end as category
    from sql.product;
```

```
                                                                    1
        PRODNAME    CATEGORY
        ------------------------
        flippers    cheap
        jet ski     outrageous
        kayak       not-so-cheap
        raft        cheap
        snorkel     cheap
        surfboard   expensive
        windsurfer  outrageous
```

See also "UPDATE Statement" for another example with a CASE expression.

See Also
sql-expression

column-definition

defines the SQL procedure's data types and dates.

Format
Each of the following is a valid form of column-definition:

column CHARACTER | VARCHAR <(*width*)>
    <column-modifier < column-modifier>... >
column INTEGER | SMALLINT
    <column-modifier <, column-modifier>... >
column DECIMAL | NUMERIC | FLOAT <(*width* <, *ndec*>)>
    <column-modifier < column-modifier>... >
column REAL | DOUBLE PRECISION
    <column-modifier < column-modifier>... >
column DATE <column-modifier>

Description
The SAS System supports many but not all of the data types that SQL-based databases do. The SQL procedure defaults to the SAS data types NUM and CHAR.

The optional *width* field on a character column specifies the width of that column; it defaults to eight characters. The SQL procedure ignores a *width* field on a numeric column. All numeric columns are created with the maximum precision allowed by the SAS System. If you want to create numeric columns that use less storage space, you can use the LENGTH statement in the SAS DATA step.

The CHARACTER, INTEGER, and DECIMAL data types can be abbreviated to CHAR, INT, and DEC, respectively.

A column declared with DATE is a SAS numeric variable with a date informat or format. You can use any of the column-modifiers to set the appropriate attributes for the column being defined. See *SAS Language: Reference* for more information on dates.

Example

```
proc sql;
create table coldefex
   (x int,
    y char(20),
    z dec(5,2)  format=comma5.2  label='Z Value'
   );

proc contents data=coldefex;
run;
```

Running the CONTENTS procedure displays information about your table in SAS output. (This procedure was run under the MVS/XA host system on an IBM computer; results may vary from system to system.)

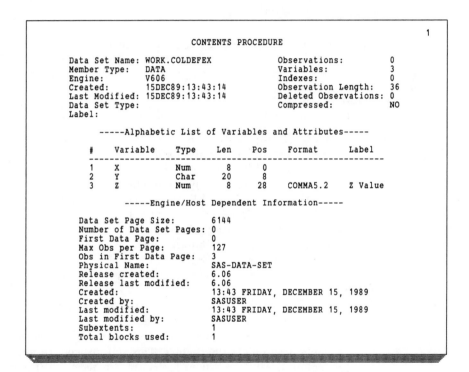

```
                                                                    1
                          CONTENTS PROCEDURE
     Data Set Name: WORK.COLDEFEX        Observations:           0
     Member Type:   DATA                 Variables:              3
     Engine:        V606                 Indexes:                0
     Created:       15DEC89:13:43:14     Observation Length:     36
     Last Modified: 15DEC89:13:43:14     Deleted Observations:   0
     Data Set Type:                      Compressed:             NO
     Label:

          -----Alphabetic List of Variables and Attributes-----

       #    Variable    Type    Len    Pos    Format      Label
       -------------------------------------------------------------
       1    X           Num      8      0
       2    Y           Char    20      8
       3    Z           Num      8     28    COMMA5.2    Z Value

             -----Engine/Host Dependent Information-----

     Data Set Page Size:      6144
     Number of Data Set Pages: 0
     First Data Page:         0
     Max Obs per Page:        127
     Obs in First Data Page:  3
     Physical Name:           SAS-DATA-SET
     Release created:         6.06
     Release last modified:   6.06
     Created:                 13:43 FRIDAY, DECEMBER 15, 1989
     Created by:              SASUSER
     Last modified:           13:43 FRIDAY, DECEMBER 15, 1989
     Last modified by:        SASUSER
     Subextents:              1
     Total blocks used:       1
```

See Also
column-modifier

column-modifier

sets column attributes.

Format

<**INFORMAT**=*informatw.d*>
<**FORMAT**=*formatw.d*>
<**LABEL**='*label*'>

Description

The INFORMAT= column-modifier alters the way SAS procedures process input to a table or SAS/ACCESS view. The LABEL= and FORMAT= column-modifiers alter the way a query-expression displays a column (heading) or its values in a result table. You can specify one or more of the column-modifiers in any order. The column attributes type and length are set in the column-definition. See "column-definition" earlier in this chapter.

The column-modifier INFORMAT= specifies the informat to be used when the SAS System accesses data from a table or SAS/ACCESS view. You can change one permanent informat to another using the ALTER statement. The SQL procedure does not use the INFORMAT= modifier: it stores informats in its table definitions so that other SAS procedures and the DATA step can use this information when they reference tables created by the SQL procedure.

The column-modifier FORMAT= determines how character and numeric values in a column are displayed by the query-expression. If the FORMAT= modifier is used in the ALTER, CREATE TABLE, or CREATE VIEW statements, it specifies the permanent format to be used when the SAS System displays data from that table or view. You can change one permanent format to another using the ALTER statement.

See Chapter 13, "SAS Informats," and Chapter 14, "SAS Formats," in *SAS Language: Reference* for more information on informats and formats. Chapter 18, "The FORMAT procedure," in the *SAS Procedures Guide* describes other uses of the formats.

The column-modifier LABEL= associates a label with a column heading. If the LABEL= modifier is used in the ALTER, CREATE TABLE, or CREATE VIEW statements, it specifies the permanent label to be used when displaying that column heading from the specified table or view. You can change one permanent label to another by using the ALTER statement. If you refer to a labeled column in the ORDER BY or GROUP BY clause, you must use either the column name (not its label), the column's alias, or its ordering integer (for example, **ORDER BY** 2). See "LABEL Statement" in *SAS Language: Reference* for more information on labels.

A label can begin with the following characters: a through z, A through Z, 0 through 9, or a space. If you begin a label with a special character, such as #, the special character does not appear in the output. If you need to start the label with a special character, precede it with a space or a slash. For example, the following labels display the special character # in the output:

```
qty label=" # of items"
qty label="/# of items"
```

See "SQL Procedure and SAS Data Set Options" earlier in this chapter for information on how you can use SAS data set options to modify column names and make other enhancements.

Example

This example creates an inventory table for a fish market. The FORMAT= column-modifier displays the data in a consistent form across the rows.

```
proc sql;
create table sql.fish
   (name char(12),                 /* fish by its common name */
    qty num informat=comma5.,      /* number of fish received */
    weight num informat=comma5.2,  /*  weight in pounds */
    datein date,                   /* date when fish received */
    sellby date                    /* date fish must be sold by */
   );

insert into sql.fish
   values('flounder',100,50,'2jun1989'd,'7 jun89'd)
   values('red snapper',20,14,'1 jun 89'd,'4jun89'd)
   values('shrimp',.,98,'3jun1989'd,'6jun 89'd)
   values('scallops',.,70,'2-jun-89'd,'6jun89'd)
   ;
```

When using a date value as a constant, you need to enclose it with single quotes and follow it with a D (for date). Notice that the numeric missing values are specified with a period.

Once you have created the Fish table and added rows of data to it, you can use labels and formats to display a report.

```
select name, qty as quantity, weight format=comma5.2,
       datein label='Date Rec''d',
       sellby label='Last Fresh Day'
   from sql.fish;
```

```
                                             Last        1
                                   Date     Fresh
    NAME          QUANTITY  WEIGHT  Rec'd     Day
    ------------------------------------------------
    flounder          100   50.00  02JUN89  07JUN89
    red snapper        20   14.00  01JUN89  04JUN89
    shrimp              .   98.00  03JUN89  06JUN89
    scallops            .   70.00  02JUN89  06JUN89
```

If you need an apostrophe (') in the label, type it twice so that the SAS System reads the apostrophe as a literal. Or, you can use single and double quotes alternately, for example, "Date Rec'd".

See Also

column-definition, object-item

column-name

defines the valid forms of a column name.

Format
Each of the following is a valid form of column-name:

column
table.column
table-alias.column
view.column
view-alias.column
sas-access-view.column
sas-access-view-alias.column

Description
A column can be referred to by its name alone if it is the only column by that name in all the tables, PROC SQL views, or SAS/ACCESS views listed in the current query-expression. For example, CUSTCITY is unique in this query:

```
select custcity from sql.customer;
```

If the same column name exists in more than one table* in the query expression, you must *qualify* each use of the column with its table name or a table alias to avoid ambiguous references. For example, when the Employee and Invoice tables are joined over the EMPNUM column, you need to distinguish the references to EMPNUM in each table. You qualify a column name by linking it with a table name, using either the table name itself (minus its libref) or an alias for that table. For example, the EMPNUM column is qualified with its table name in this query:

```
select employee.empnum, empname, prodname, invqty, invprice
   from sql.employee, sql.invoice
   where employee.empnum=invoice.empnum;
```

Tables aliases are described in "from-list" later in this chapter and are shown in the second example in the following section.

Examples
The first example shows how to calculate and list the difference between the cost of a product and its list price. Notice that there would be no column name for the result of the arithmetic expression unless a column alias or label is used for

---

* For simplicity, *table* is used in this description to mean *table, PROC SQL view,* or *SAS/ACCESS view.*

it. The FORMAT= modifier makes the values in the COSTDIFF column look like those in the other columns.

```
proc sql;
select prodname as product, prodcost, prodlist,
        (prodlist-prodcost) as costdiff format=dollar.
    from sql.product
    order by costdiff;
```

```
                                                             1
           PRODUCT   PRODCOST  PRODLIST  COSTDIFF
           ----------------------------------------
           raft            $5        $7        $2
           snorkel        $12       $15        $3
           flippers       $16       $20        $4
           kayak         $190      $240       $50
           surfboard     $615      $750      $135
           windsurfer  $1,090    $1,325      $235
           jet ski     $2,150    $2,675      $525
```

Notice that a column alias is not case-sensitive. That is, regardless of the case (lower, upper, or mixed) in which you type it, the alias is output in uppercase. To define the output case, you must use a LABEL= modifier.

You can also write the ORDER BY clause as follows, where an integer reflecting the column's ordinal position in the SELECT list achieves the same result:

```
order by 4;
```

In this next example, you can join a table with itself to get a report of sales representatives and their managers, together with the cities in which they live. The table aliases REP and MGR are used to qualify the columns in the SELECT list. The column aliases MANAGER and MGRCITY make the table's results clearer to the reader. Notice that the AS keyword is required with column alias specifications but is optional when you specify table aliases.

```
title 'Sales Representatives';
select rep.empname label='Sales Representative',
       rep.empcity, mgr.empname as manager,
       mgr.empcity as mgrcity
    from sql.employee rep, sql.employee mgr
    where rep.empboss=mgr.empnum and rep.emptitle='salesrep';
```

```
                    Sales Representatives                        1
    Sales
    Representative  EMPCITY         MANAGER  MGRCITY
    -----------------------------------------------------------
    Joe             Virginia Beach  Betty    Ocean City
    Jeff            Virginia Beach  Betty    Ocean City
    Wanda           Ocean City      Betty    Ocean City
    Fred            Ocean City      Betty    Ocean City
    Marvin          Wilmington      Sally    Wilmington
    Nick            Myrtle Beach    Sally    Wilmington
    Sam             Charleston      Chuck    Charleston
```

See Also
column-modifier, object-item, table-name

exists-condition

tests if a subquery returns one or more rows.

Format

<NOT> **EXISTS** (query-expression)

Description
The EXISTS condition is an operator whose right operand is a subquery. The result of an EXISTS condition is true if the subquery evaluates to at least one row. The result of a NOT EXISTS condition is true if the subquery evaluates to zero rows.

Example
To find employees who did not make any sales, you can use an EXISTS condition together with a correlated subquery. Here is a a step-by-step description of how this query executes. For each employee in the Employee table, extract a list of invoices recorded as being made by that employee. If that list is empty (it doesn't exist), then select this employee for display.

```
proc sql;
select empname, 'is a poor sales representative'
   from sql.employee
   where not exists (select *
                         from sql.invoice
                         where empnum=employee.empnum)
        and emptitle='salesrep';
```

```
                                                                      1
          EMPNAME
          ------------------------------------------
          Jeff      is a poor sales representative
```

See "sql-expression" for more information on correlated subqueries.

See Also

query-expression

---

from-list

specifies source tables, views, or SAS/ACCESS views in a FROM clause.

Format

Each of the following is a valid form of from-list:

table-name <<**AS**> *alias*>
  <*libref.*>*view* <<**AS**> *alias*>
  <*libref.*>*sas-access-view* <<**AS**> *alias*>
  joined-table
  (query-expression) <<**AS** > *alias*
                    <(column-name <, column-name>...)>>

Description

The FROM clause is used in a query-expression to specify the table(s) from which you retrieve data.* When multiple tables are specified, the SQL procedure combines or *joins* the tables to form one result table. A table can also be joined with itself. See "joined-table" later in this chapter for more information on joining tables in the FROM clause.

A table alias is a temporary, alternate name for a table that is specified in the FROM clause. Table aliases are used to qualify column names so that the correct columns are processed when tables are joined. Table aliases are always required when joining a table with itself; column names in other kinds of joins must be qualified with table aliases or table names unless the column names are unique in those tables.

The keyword AS is often used to distinguish a table alias from other table names. This keyword is optional and can be omitted.

In-line views   The FROM clause can itself contain a query-expression that takes an optional table alias. This kind of nested query-expression is called an *in-line view*. An in-line view is any query-expression that would be valid in a CREATE VIEW statement. The SQL procedure can support many levels of nesting but is limited to 16 tables in any one query.

An in-line view saves you a coding step: rather than creating a view and referring to it in another query (two steps), you can code the view *in-line* in the

---

* For simplicity, *table* is used in this description to mean *table, PROC SQL view,* or *SAS/ACCESS view.*

FROM clause. An in-line view is not assigned a permanent name (although it can take an alias), and it can be referred to only in the query in which it is defined; that is, an in-line view cannot be referenced in another query. You cannot use an ORDER BY clause in an in-line view.

The names of columns in an in-line view can be assigned in the object-item list of that view or with a parenthesized list of names following the table alias.

Examples

This example joins the Employee and Invoice tables. The query lists employees whose employee numbers are under 300 and the sales they have made. Table aliases defined in the FROM clause are used throughout the query to distinguish the column references.

```
proc sql;
   select e.empnum, e.empname, prodname, invqty, invprice
      from sql.employee as e, sql.invoice as i
      where e.empnum=i.empnum and e.empnum<300
      order by e.empname;
```

```
                                                              1
     EMPNUM  EMPNAME  PRODNAME    INVQTY  INVPRICE
     --------------------------------------------------
        216  Fred     flippers        15       $19
        216  Fred     raft            20        $7
        213  Joe      surfboard        4      $735
        213  Joe      snorkel         15       $15
        213  Joe      snorkel         10       $15
        213  Joe      raft            10        $7
        215  Wanda    flippers        10       $20
        215  Wanda    flippers         5       $20
        215  Wanda    snorkel         20       $14
```

This example lists products that were not sold to stores in Myrtle Beach by sales representatives who live in Virginia Beach. It lists products that did not sell, that is, flippers, kayaks, surfboards, and windsurfers.

```
select distinct prodname
   from   sql.invoice
   where prodname not in
         (select table1.prodname
             from (select distinct prodname
                      from  sql.customer as c, sql.invoice as i
                      where c.custname=i.custname and
                            c.custnum=i.custnum and
                            c.custcity='Myrtle Beach') as table1,
                   (select distinct prodname
                      from  sql.invoice as i, sql.employee as e
                      where e.empnum=i.empnum and
                            e.empcity='Virginia Beach') as table2
             where table1.prodname=table2.prodname)
      order by 1;
```

```
                                                              1
            PRODNAME
            ----------
            flippers
            kayak
            surfboard
            windsurfer
```

This example contains two in-line views that are nested in a subquery. To understand this query, first look at how each in-line view is evaluated. Table1, the first in-line view, returns all the products sold in Myrtle Beach. Table2, the second in-line view, returns all the products sold by employees who live in Virginia Beach. The SELECT clause in the subquery then chooses products that are common to both Table1 and Table2. You now have a list of products to which you can apply the WHERE expression of the outermost query; this expression displays the products NOT IN the list that was just derived.

See Also
column-name, CREATE statement, joined-table, query-expression, table-name

---

group-by-item

specifies the groups of column values that the summary function processes in a GROUP BY clause.

Format
Each of the following is a valid form of group-by-item:

integer
column-name
sql-expression

Description
The GROUP BY clause is used in query-expressions that include one or more summary functions. It applies the summary function to the values in each column (or group-by-item) specified in the GROUP BY clause. The GROUP BY clause is shown in "table-expression" later in this chapter.

A summary function is one of the operands that can be included in an sql-expression, but a group-by-item cannot be a summary function. Summary functions can only be included in the SELECT and HAVING clauses of a query-expression.

For example, this query calculates the average number of years of service by each job title and how many employees there are, according to job title. Thus, the AVG function is applied to each group of column values (EMPYEARS) and returns one row for each job title in the table, and FREQ is applied to each group of EMPNUM values and returns a row with the number of employees per

job title. The averages are displayed as whole numbers by means of the
FORMAT=6.0 column-modifier.

```
proc sql;
select emptitle as title,
       avg(empyears) label='Average Years' format=6.0,
       freq(empnum) label='Head Count'
   from sql.employee
   group by title
   order by title;
```

```
                                                                    1
                       Average     Head
              TITLE      Years     Count
              -----------------------------
              manager      10         3
              president    28         1
              salesrep      5         7
```

Multiple group-by-items are separated by commas. You can specify more
than one group-by-item to get more detail, for example, to group values in a
result table by the sales representatives' sales and the city in which the sales
took place. This grouping of multiple items is evaluated in a manner similar to
that in the BY statement of a PROC step. If more than one group-by-item is
specified, the first one determines the major grouping.

Integers can be substituted for column names (that is, SELECT object-items)
in the GROUP BY clause. If the group-by-item is an integer (say 2), the results
are grouped by the values in the second column of the SELECT clause list. Using
integers can shorten your coding and enables you to group by the value of an
unnamed expression in the SELECT list.

The data do not have to be sorted in the order of the group-by values
because the SQL procedure handles sorting automatically. You can use the
ORDER BY clause to specify the order in which rows are displayed in the result
table.

If you specify a GROUP BY clause in a query that does not contain a
summary function, your clause is transformed into an ORDER BY clause and a
message to that effect is written to the SAS log.

It is invalid to group by a column that contains a summary function in the
sql-expression. For example, the following GROUP BY clause is invalid:

```
group by sum(x)
```

Example

This query lists customers who have four stores and those stores' numbers. In the subquery, the COUNT(*) function is used to count the stores. They are then grouped by each customer's name.

```
proc sql;
select custname as customer, custnum, custcity
   from  sql.customer
   where custname in
          (select custname
                from sql.customer
                group by custname
                having count(*)=4)
   order  by 1,2;
```

```
                                                                    1
        CUSTOMER     CUSTNUM  CUSTCITY
        ----------------------------------------
        Coast Shop         3  Myrtle Beach
        Coast Shop         5  Myrtle Beach
        Coast Shop        12  Virginia Beach
        Coast Shop        14  Charleston
        Surf Mart        101  Charleston
        Surf Mart        118  Surfside
        Surf Mart        127  Ocean Isle
        Surf Mart        133  Charleston
```

Notice that a column alias (for example, CUSTOMER) can only be a single word; if you need more than one word, you should use a label. See "column-modifier" elsewhere in this chapter for a description of the LABEL= column-modifier and its use.

See Also
column-name, sql-expression, summary-function

---

having-expression

specifies a condition that each group in the query must satisfy.

Format

HAVING sql-expression

Description

The HAVING expression is any valid SQL expression that is evaluated once for each group in a query; if the query involves remerged data, the HAVING expression is evaluated for each row participating in each group. The query must include one or more summary functions.

When specified, the GROUP BY clause precedes the HAVING expression and defines the group(s) to be evaluated. If the HAVING expression evaluates to true for a group, that group will be processed further. Otherwise, the SQL procedure stops processing that group and begins processing the next one, if multiple groups are defined by the values of the GROUP BY clause.

If no GROUP BY clause is specified, the expression is evaluated as if the items listed in the SELECT clause were all in one group. That is, when the expression in the HAVING clause evaluates to true, all the items listed in the SELECT clause are displayed in the result table. If false, the items are not displayed.

Examples
This query first counts the total number of stores (using COUNT(*)) that each customer has (applying the GROUP BY clause). The HAVING expression then selects the row(s) that satisfy its condition, that is, the customer with only one store. The customer who has one store is then displayed.

```
proc sql;
select custname as name, count(*)
   from sql.customer
   group by name
   having count(*)=1;
```

```
                                                              1
              NAME
              --------------------
              Beach Land        1
```

In the next example of a query with a HAVING expression, the results of the summary function are redistributed across the rows (that is, original data) of the source table. This example lists the employees, grouped by their job titles, that have worked more than the average number of years for their particular job title.

```
select empname, emptitle, empyears
   from sql.employee
   group by emptitle
   having empyears>avg(empyears);
```

The SQL procedure may not perform each of the following steps exactly as described because of its optimizer, but the following steps can help you conceptualize the process.

In the SQL procedure's first pass through the data, it groups the rows into three categories, according to each employee's EMPTITLE. It then calculates the average number of EMPYEARS per category. This internal arrangement and the average years per job title are shown here:

EMPNAME	EMPTITLE	EMPYEARS	avg(empyears)
Sally	manager	9	
Betty	manager	8	
Chuck	manager	12	9.66
Herb	president	28	28
Fred	salesrep	6	
Wanda	salesrep	10	
Nick	salesrep	1	
Marvin	salesrep	5	
Jeff	salesrep	1	
Sam	salesrep	7	
Joe	salesrep	2	4.57

In the procedure's second pass through the data, the HAVING expression is evaluated and the data from the original table (EMPYEARS) are remerged back with the results of the summary function. That is, the HAVING expression compares the EMPYEARS value for each row in the table (and EMPYEARS changes with each row) with the average number of years worked for each job title (a constant value). When an employee's number of years worked is greater than the average for the job title, the expression evaluates to true for that row.

EMPNAME	EMPTITLE	EMPYEARS	avg(empyears)	having
Sally	manager	9	9.66	FALSE
Betty	manager	8	9.66	FALSE
Chuck	manager	12	9.66	TRUE
Herb	president	28	28	FALSE
Fred	salesrep	6	4.57	TRUE
Wanda	salesrep	10	4.57	TRUE
Nick	salesrep	1	4.57	FALSE
Marvin	salesrep	5	4.57	TRUE
Jeff	salesrep	1	4.57	FALSE
Sam	salesrep	7	4.57	TRUE
Joe	salesrep	2	4.57	FALSE

When the evaluations are completed, the rows for which the HAVING expression evaluates to true are displayed in the final output table. A message is written to the SAS log to make you aware that remerging with the original data has occurred.

```
NOTE: The query requires remerging the summary statistics
      back with the original data.
```

```
                                                              1
          EMPNAME   EMPTITLE   EMPYEARS
          ----------------------------
          Chuck     manager          12
          Fred      salesrep          6
          Wanda     salesrep         10
          Marvin    salesrep          5
          Sam       salesrep          7
```

See "summary-function" later in this chapter for more information on evaluating summary functions with nonsummary expressions.

See Also
sql-expression, summary-function

host-variable

stores the value of a column for use later in another PROC SQL query or SAS procedure.

Format

:macrovariable

Description
Many SQL products allow the embedding of SQL into another language, and references to variables (columns) of that language are termed *host-variable references*. They are differentiated from references to columns in tables by names that are prefixed with a colon. The host-variable stores the values of the object-items listed in the SELECT clause.

Currently, the only host language available is the macro language, which is part of the macro facility in base SAS software. When a calculation is performed on a column's value, its result is stored—using *:macro-variable*—in the macro facility. The result can then be referenced by that name in another PROC SQL query or SAS procedure. Host-variable stores the values of the object-items listed in the SELECT clause. Host-variable can only be used in the outer query of a SELECT statement, not in a subquery.

If the query produces more than one row of output, the macro variable will contain only the value from the first row. If the query has no rows in its output, the macro variables are not modified or, if they did not exist yet, they are not created. You can check the PROC SQL macro variable SQLOBS to see the number of rows produced by the query-expression. See "Macro Variables Set by Statements in the SQL Procedure" earlier in this chapter.

Example

A useful feature of host variables is that they enable you to display data values in SAS titles. The following query prints the Invoice table with a title that reflects the largest sale:

```
proc sql;
reset noprint;
select max(invqty*invprice)
   into :maxsale
   from sql.invoice;

reset print;
title "The Best Sale Totalled &maxsale";
select * from sql.invoice;
```

```
                    The Best Sale Totalled    2940                          1

    INVNUM  CUSTNAME   CUSTNUM   EMPNUM  PRODNAME    INVQTY  INVPRICE
    --------------------------------------------------------------------
       280  Beach Land     16      215  snorkel         20      $14
       290  Beach Land     16      216  flippers        15      $19
       300  Beach Land     16      216  raft            20       $7
       310  Coast Shop      3      318  windsurfer       2   $1,305
       320  Coast Shop      3      318  raft            30       $6
       330  Coast Shop      5      318  snorkel          5      $15
       340  Coast Shop      5      318  flippers        15      $19
       350  Coast Shop      5      318  raft            40       $6
       360  Coast Shop      5      318  snorkel         10      $15
       370  Coast Shop     12      213  raft            10       $7
       380  Coast Shop     14      417  windsurfer       1   $1,325
       390  Del Mar         3      417  flippers        30      $18
       400  Del Mar         3      417  kayak            3     $230
       410  Del Mar         8      417  raft            40       $6
       420  Del Mar        11      417  raft            15       $7
       430  Del Mar        11      417  snorkel         10      $15
       440  Del Mar        11      417  flippers        20      $19
       450  New Waves       3      215  flippers         5      $20
       460  New Waves       3      215  flippers        10      $20
       470  New Waves       6      213  snorkel         15      $15
       480  New Waves       6      213  surfboard        4     $735
       490  New Waves       6      213  snorkel         10      $15
       500  Surf Mart     101      417  snorkel         20      $14
       510  Surf Mart     101      417  surfboard        2     $740
       520  Surf Mart     101      417  snorkel         12      $15
       530  Surf Mart     118      318  flippers        15      $19
       540  Surf Mart     118      318  raft            30       $6
       550  Surf Mart     118      318  snorkel         10      $15
       560  Surf Mart     127      314  flippers        25      $19
       570  Surf Mart     127      314  surfboard        3     $740
```

See Also

object-item

in-condition

tests set membership.

Format
Each of the following is a valid form of in-condition:

sql-expression <NOT> **IN** (*constant* <, *constant*>...)
sql-expression <NOT> **IN** (query-expression)

Description
An IN condition tests if the column value returned by the sql-expression on the left is a member of the set (of constants or values returned by the query-expression) on the right. If so, it selects rows based upon the column value. That is, the IN condition is true if the value of the left operand is in the set of values defined by the right operand. The IN condition can be used in any sql-expression.

Examples
This example displays employees who live in Wilmington or Charleston, using a list of constants as the membership set.

```
proc sql;
title 'Who Lives in Wilmington or Charleston?';
select empname
   from sql.employee
   where empcity in ('Wilmington', 'Charleston');
```

```
           Who Lives in Wilmington or Charleston?              1

                          EMPNAME
                          --------
                          Sally
                          Marvin
                          Chuck
                          Sam
```

The next example uses an IN condition in the SELECT clause of the query. In this case, the IN condition lists all the rows that can be selected and evaluates each for a true (1) or false (0) value. (This evaluation is consistent with other SAS conventions where the result of a Boolean expression is always 1 or 0.) If this query were rewritten and the IN condition appeared in the WHERE clause, only the rows with **Wilmington** and **Charleston** would be selected for the output table.

```
select distinct empcity,
      empcity in ('Wilmington','Charleston')
   from sql.employee;
```

```
                                                                   1
                EMPCITY
                ------------------------
                Ocean City              0
                Virginia Beach          0
                Wilmington              1
                Myrtle Beach            0
                Charleston              1
```

The next example finds all the cities in which no manager lives. To do this search, you must first use a subquery to find all the cities that have managers living in them. The values of those rows are then returned to the outer query.

```
title 'Which Cities Have No Manager?';
select distinct empcity
   from sql.employee
   where empcity not in (select empcity
                            from sql.employee
                            where emptitle='manager');
```

This subquery returns `Ocean City`, `Wilmington`, and `Charleston`, so the IN condition processes the outer query as follows:

```
where empcity not in ('Ocean City','Wilmington','Charleston');
```

The result table of the query lists the two remaining cities in the set as specified by the EMPCITY column.

```
            Which Cities Have No Manager?               1
                   EMPCITY
                   ---------------
                   Virginia Beach
                   Myrtle Beach
```

See Also
query-expression, sql-expression

is-condition

tests for a missing value.

Format
Each of the following is a valid form of is-condition:

sql-expression **IS** <NOT> **NULL**
sql-expression **IS** <NOT> **MISSING**

Description
IS NULL and IS MISSING are predicates that test for a missing value; they are used in the WHERE, ON, and HAVING expressions. Each predicate evaluates to true if the sql-expression's result is missing and false if it is not.

The SAS System stores a numeric missing value as a period (.) and a character missing value as a blank space. Unlike some versions of SQL, missing values in the SAS System always come first in the collating sequence. Therefore, in Boolean and comparison operations, the following expressions evaluate to true in a predicate:

```
 3>null
-3>null
 0>null
```

The SAS System's way of evaluating missing values differs from that of the ANSI Standard for SQL; according to the Standard, these expressions would be NULL. See "sql-expression" later in this chapter for more information on predicates and operators; see Appendix 2, "SQL Procedure and the ANSI Standard for SQL," for more information on the ANSI Standard.

Example

The following example returns employees who have no boss:

```
proc sql;
title 'Who Has No Boss?';
select *
   from sql.employee
   where empboss is null;
```

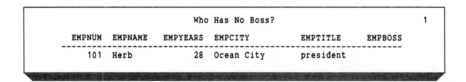

See *SAS Language: Reference* for more information on missing (or NULL) values.

See Also

sql-expression

joined-table

joins a table with itself or with other tables.

Format

Each of the following is a valid form of joined-table:

table <<**AS**> *alias*>, *table* <<**AS**> *alias*>
  <, *table* <<**AS**> *alias*>... >
table <**INNER**> **JOIN** *table* **ON** sql-expression
table **LEFT JOIN** *table* **ON** sql-expression
table **RIGHT JOIN** *table* **ON** sql-expression
table **FULL JOIN** *table* **ON** sql-expression

    where *table* can be any one of the following:

table-name
<*libref.*>*view*
<*libref.*>*sas-access-view*
query-expression

Description

The FROM clause is used in a query-expression to specify the table(s), PROC SQL view(s), SAS/ACCESS view(s), or query-expression(s) from which you retrieve data. If more than one of these are listed in the FROM clause, they are joined to form one output table. These queries are commonly called *join queries* or, more simply, *joins*. The first two formats listed in the previous section are inner joins, and the last three are outer joins.

    According to the conceptual model, when two tables are specified,* each row of table A is matched with all the rows of table B to produce an internal or intermediate table. The number of rows in the intermediate table (*Cartesian product*) is equal to the product of the number of rows in each of the source tables. The intermediate table becomes the input to the rest of the query where some of its rows may be eliminated by the WHERE expression or summarized by a summary function.

    The WHERE clause or ON clause contains the conditions (sql-expression) under which the rows in the Cartesian product are kept or eliminated in the result table. An sql-expression can be any operand listed in the "sql-expression" description except a summary function. The expression is evaluated for each row from each table in the intermediate table described earlier. The row is considered matching if the result of the expression is true (a nonzero, nonmissing value) for that row.

    An *equijoin* between two (or more) tables has a condition in the sql-expression in which the value of a column in the first table must equal the value of a column in the second. The SAS System processes equijoins by sorting the two tables and merging the data by their matching values. If an index is defined on the column being matched in the equijoin, tables may not have to be sorted before merging the data by their matching values; that is, the sorting is optional. See "Role of Indexes in Equijoins" in Chapter 4 for information on

---

* For simplicity, *table* is used in the rest of this description to mean *table, PROC SQL view, SAS/ACCESS view,* or *query-expression.* A query-expression in the FROM clause is usually referred to as an *in-line view.* See "from-list" for more information on in-line views.

using indexes to improve query performance. Equijoins can be inner or outer joins.

Table aliases are used in joins to distinguish the columns of one table from those in the other table(s). A qualifying table name or table alias is required whenever joined tables have matching column names in the query. See "from-list" earlier in this chapter for more information on table aliases.

Joining a table with itself   A single table can be joined with itself to produce more information. These joins are sometimes called *reflexive joins*. In these joins, the same table is listed twice in the FROM clause. Both tables must be given a table alias or you will not be able to distinguish between references to columns in either instance of the table.

Inner joins   A *conventional* join, or *inner join*, returns a result table for all the rows in a table that has one or more matching rows in the other table(s), as specified by the sql-expression. Inner joins can be performed on up to 16 tables in a query-expression.

An inner join is the only form of join that many products based on SQL support. You can perform an inner join by using a comma-separated list of table-names or by using the <INNER> JOIN and ON keywords; both forms are illustrated later in this section.

The Cartesian product effect of SQL joins is demonstrated by key value 2 in the following examples. It appears twice on both the Left and the Right tables and thus four times in the output produced by a join query. The system determines the order of the rows, which may vary as the sizes of the tables change or as columns have indexes defined on them. To set a particular order in the result table, you must use the ORDER BY clause.

Notice that a DATA step is used to create the example's data sets, although the SQL procedure processes the data. The SQL procedure can process any SAS data set, regardless of the procedure that created it.

```
data sql.left;
   length key 4 lname $12 lcity $12;
   input key lname lcity;
   cards;
1 Lewis Durham
2 Cummings Raleigh
2 Kent Cary
3 Eaton Durham
;

proc sql;
title 'Left Table';
select * from sql.left;
```

```
                          Left Table                         1

                    KEY  LNAME        LCITY
                  --------------------------------------
                      1  Lewis        Durham
                      2  Cummings     Raleigh
                      2  Kent         Cary
                      3  Eaton        Durham
```

```
data sql.right;
    length key 4 rname $12 rcity $12;
    input key rname rcity;
    cards;
1 Johnston Durham
2 Dean Cary
2 Corrigan Raleigh
4 Gomez Cary
;

proc sql;
title 'Right Table';
select * from sql.right;
```

```
                          Right Table                        1

                    KEY  RNAME        RCITY
                  --------------------------------------
                      1  Johnston     Durham
                      2  Dean         Cary
                      2  Corrigan     Raleigh
                      4  Gomez        Cary
```

The Left and Right tables can be joined using either the INNER JOIN and ON keywords or a table-name list (shown in the next example). Both forms of the query produce the same results. Notice that the column names are qualified with the table names so that the correct columns can be processed. An equijoin is performed here because the values in the KEY column of each table are matched.

```
title 'Inner Join';
select *
    from sql.left inner join sql.right
        on left.key=right.key;
```

```
                           Inner Join                              1
        KEY  LNAME          LCITY          KEY  RNAME        RCITY
       ------------------------------------------------------------------
          1  Lewis          Durham           1  Johnston     Durham
          2  Cummings       Raleigh          2  Dean         Cary
          2  Cummings       Raleigh          2  Corrigan     Raleigh
          2  Kent           Cary             2  Dean         Cary
          2  Kent           Cary             2  Corrigan     Raleigh
```

Next, the tables are joined using a table-name list to produce the same results. This form of an inner join is the one more frequently used.

```
proc sql;
title 'Inner Join';
select *
   from sql.left, sql.right
   where left.key=right.key;
```

Outer joins   Outer joins are inner joins that have been augmented with rows that did not match with any row from the other table in the join. Outer joins can be performed on only two tables at a time. Outer joins are of three kinds: left, right, and full. Equijoins are performed in each outer join example because the values in the KEY column of each table are matched.

A left outer join, specified with the keywords LEFT JOIN and ON, has all the rows from the Cartesian product of the two tables for which the sql-expression is true, plus rows from the first (Left) table that do not match any row in the Right table.

```
title 'Left Outer Join';
select *
   from sql.left left join sql.right
   on left.key=right.key;
```

```
                         Left Outer Join                          1
        KEY  LNAME          LCITY          KEY  RNAME        RCITY
       ------------------------------------------------------------------
          1  Lewis          Durham           1  Johnston     Durham
          2  Kent           Cary             2  Corrigan     Raleigh
          2  Cummings       Raleigh          2  Corrigan     Raleigh
          2  Kent           Cary             2  Dean         Cary
          2  Cummings       Raleigh          2  Dean         Cary
          3  Eaton          Durham                  .
```

A right outer join, specified with the keywords RIGHT JOIN and ON, has all the rows from the Cartesian product of the two tables for which the sql-expression is true, plus rows from the second (Right) table that do not match any row in the first (Left) table.

```
title 'Right Outer Join';
select *
   from sql.left right join sql.right
   on left.key=right.key;
```

```
                            Right Outer Join                              1

     KEY  LNAME        LCITY            KEY  RNAME        RCITY
     --------------------------------------------------------------------
       1  Lewis        Durham             1  Johnston     Durham
       2  Kent         Cary               2  Corrigan     Raleigh
       2  Kent         Cary               2  Dean         Cary
       2  Cummings     Raleigh            2  Corrigan     Raleigh
       2  Cummings     Raleigh            2  Dean         Cary
       .                                  4  Gomez        Cary
```

A full outer join, specified with the keywords FULL JOIN and ON, has all
the rows from the Cartesian product of the two tables for which the
sql-expression is true, plus rows from each table that do not match any row in
the other table.

```
title 'Full Outer Join';
select *
   from sql.left full join sql.right
   on left.key=right.key;
```

```
                            Full Outer Join                              1

     KEY  LNAME        LCITY            KEY  RNAME        RCITY
     --------------------------------------------------------------------
       1  Lewis        Durham             1  Johnston     Durham
       2  Kent         Cary               2  Corrigan     Raleigh
       2  Kent         Cary               2  Dean         Cary
       2  Cummings     Raleigh            2  Corrigan     Raleigh
       2  Cummings     Raleigh            2  Dean         Cary
       3  Eaton        Durham             .
       .                                  4  Gomez        Cary
```

Joining more than two tables   Joins are usually performed on two or three
tables, but they can be performed on up to 16 tables in the SQL procedure. A
join on three tables is described here so you can understand how and why the
relationships work among the tables.

In a three-way join, the sql-expression consists of two conditions: one relates
the first table to the second table and one relates the second table to the third
table. For example, this query lists who sold windsurfers and at what cost. You
start with the Invoice table to see who sold windsurfers. You then
cross-reference the Employee table to obtain the employee names from the
employee numbers recorded in Invoice table. The cross reference to the Product
table then gives you a windsurfer's cost, so you can multiply it by the quantity of
windsurfers sold.

```
proc sql;
select e.empname, i.custname, i.prodname, i.invqty,
       i.invqty*p.prodcost label='Cost Price' format=dollar.
    from sql.invoice i, sql.employee e, sql.product p
    where i.prodname='windsurfer' and i.empnum=e.empnum
        and i.prodname=p.prodname;
```

```
                                                         1
                                              Cost
   EMPNAME   CUSTNAME    PRODNAME    INVQTY   Price
   -------------------------------------------------
   Nick      Coast Shop  windsurfer       2  $2,180
   Sam       Coast Shop  windsurfer       1  $1,090
```

You could break this example into stages, doing a two-way join into a temporary table and then joining that table with the third one for the same result; however, the SQL procedure enables you to do it all at once and with less code.

```
create table threej as
select e.empname, i.custname, i.prodname, i.invqty
   from sql.invoice i, sql.employee e
   where i.prodname='windsurfer'
         and i.empnum=e.empnum;

select t.*, t.invqty*p.prodcost label='Cost Price' format=dollar.
   from threej t, sql.product p
   where t.prodname=p.prodname;
```

See Also
from-list, summary-function, where-expression

---

like-condition

tests for a matching pattern.

Format

sql-expression <NOT> **LIKE** sql-expression

Description
The LIKE condition selects rows by comparing character strings with a pattern-matching specification. It returns true and displays the matched string(s) if the left operand matches the pattern specified by the right operand. Patterns are composed of three classes of characters:

_ (underscore)	matches any single character
% (percent sign)	matches any sequence of zero or more characters
any other character	matches that character.

These patterns can appear before, after, or on both sides of characters that you want to match.

The following list gives some examples for a table that contains the values: `Smith`, `Smooth`, `Smothers`, `Smart`, and `Smuggle`. Notice that the character string must be enclosed in quotes:

'Sm%'	matches `Smith, Smooth, Smothers, Smart, Smuggle`
"%th"	matches `Smith, Smooth`
'S_ _gg%'	matches `Smuggle`
"S_o"	matches a three-letterword, so it has no matches here
'S_o%'	matches `Smooth, Smothers`
'S%th'	matches `Smith, Smooth`
"Z"	matches the single, uppercase character Z only, so it has no matches here.

The LIKE condition is case-sensitive. If you want to search for strings that appear in mixed cases, you may want to use the SAS UPCASE function to make all the names uppercase before entering the LIKE condition:

```
upcase(name) like 'SM%';
```

The UPCASE function makes `smythe` and `Smith` uppercase so that the 'SM%' pattern can find both names.

Examples

This example displays customer names that begin with the letter `S`:

```
proc sql;
select distinct custname
    from sql.customer
    where custname like "S%";
```

```
                                                          1
                  CUSTNAME
                  ----------
                  Sea Sports
                  Surf Mart
```

The next example uses the NOT LIKE condition to display customer cities that do not end in `Beach`.

```
select distinct custcity
   from sql.customer
   where custcity not like '%Beach';
```

```
                                                                      1
                       CUSTCITY
                       ---------------
                       Ocean City
                       Charleston
                       Surfside
                       Ocean Isle
```

See Also
sql-expression

object-item

lists items in the SELECT clause of a query-expression.

Format
Each of the following is a valid form of object-item:

*

table.*
table-alias.*
view.*
view-alias.*
sas-access-view.*
sas-access-view-alias.*
column-name   <**AS** *alias*> <column-modifier <column-modifier>... >
sql-expression <**AS** *alias*> <column-modifier <column-modifier>... >

Description
Object items are listed in the SELECT clause of a query-expression. The asterisk (*) is a shorthand for all columns of the table(s) listed in the FROM clause. (For simplicity, *table* is used in this description to mean *table, PROC SQL view,* or *SAS/ACCESS view.*) When an asterisk is not qualified by a table name, it indicates that all the columns from all tables in the FROM clause are to be processed; when it is qualified (that is, *table.** or *table-alias.**), it indicates all the columns from that table are to be processed.

Column-name and sql-expression can take both an alias and column-modifiers (such as an informat, format, or label). For more information, see "column-name" and "sql-expression" elsewhere in this chapter.

Using a column alias   A column alias is a temporary, alternate name for a column. Aliases are specified in the SELECT clause to name or rename columns so that the result table is clearer or easier to read. Aliases are often used to name a column that is the result of an arithmetic expression or summary function, as shown in the example in the next section. An alias is one word long; if you need a longer column name, you must use the LABEL= column-modifier, as described in "column-modifier" earlier in this chapter. The keyword AS is required with a column alias to distinguish the alias from other column names in the SELECT clause.

Column aliases are optional, and if you want, each column name in the SELECT clause can have an alias. Once you give a column an alias, you can refer to that alias when listing the column in the ORDER BY and GROUP BY clauses.

If you use a column alias when creating a PROC SQL view, the alias becomes the permanent name of the column for each execution of the view. If you specify the NUMBER option in the PROC SQL statement when you create your view, you cannot order by the ROW column. See the NUMBER option described in "PROC SQL and RESET Statements" earlier in this chapter.

Example

This example uses labels to rename the columns and to give additional information about the columns' value. The DOLLAR*w.d* and COMMA*w.d* formats illustrate two of the more commonly used SAS formats.

```
proc sql;
select prodname label='Product Name',
       prodlist label='List Price of This Item' format=dollar8.0,
       prodcost label='COST PRICE (DO NOT REVEAL)' format=comma8.0
   from sql.product;
```

```
                                           1
                            List     COST
                           Price    PRICE
                Product   of This  (DO NOT
                Name         Item   REVEAL)
                -------------------------------
                flippers      $20        16
                jet ski   $2,675     2,150
                kayak        $240       190
                raft           $7         5
                snorkel       $15        12
                surfboard    $750       615
                windsurfer $1,325     1,090
```

See Also

column-definition, column-modifier, sql-expression

order-by-item

specifies in an ORDER BY clause the order in which rows are displayed in a result table.

Format
Each of the following is a valid form of order-by-item:

integer <ASC | DESC>
column-name <ASC | DESC>
sql-expression <ASC | DESC>

Description
The ORDER BY clause sorts your query expression's output according to the order specified in that query. When this clause is used, the default ordering sequence is ascending, from the lowest value to the highest. You can use the SORTSEQ= option to change the collating sequence for your output; see "PROC SQL and RESET Statements" earlier in this chapter.

An SQL table has no inherent order. If an ORDER BY clause is omitted, the SAS System's default collating sequence and your host system determine the order of a result table's rows. Therefore, if you want your result table to appear in a particular order, use the ORDER BY clause.

Using an ORDER BY clause has certain performance costs, as does any sorting procedure. If you are querying large tables and the order of their results is not important, your queries will run faster without an ORDER BY clause.

The SQL procedure allows you to specify the ORDER BY clause in the CREATE VIEW statement. Each time the view is accessed, its data are sorted and displayed in the requested order. See "CREATE Statement" earlier in this chapter for more information on creating views with an ORDER BY clause.

If more than one order-by-item is specified (separated by commas), the first one determines the major sort order. If the order-by-item is an integer (say 2), the results are ordered by the values of the second column. If a query-expression includes a set operator (for example, UNION), you should use integers to specify the order; doing so avoids ambiguous references to columns in the table expressions.

In the ORDER BY clause, you can specify any column of a table or view that is specified in the FROM clause of a query-expression, regardless of whether that column has been included in the query's SELECT clause.

Example

This query produces a report ordered by price markup (PRODLIST/PRODCOST) but does not display the column with the markup prices. This example shows that you can use an arithmetic expression in the ORDER BY clause and that you do not need to include the item ordered by in the SELECT clause. The note is written to the SAS log.

```
proc sql;
select *
   from sql.product
   order by prodlist/prodcost desc;

NOTE: The query as specified involves ordering by an item that doesn't
      appear in its SELECT clause.
```

```
                                                              1
          PRODNAME    PRODCOST  PRODLIST
          ---------------------------------
          raft              $5        $7
          kayak          $190      $240
          flippers        $16       $20
          snorkel         $12       $15
          jet ski      $2,150    $2,675
          surfboard      $615      $750
          windsurfer   $1,090    $1,325
```

In most cases, you would display the markup value for clarity.

See Also

column-name, sql-expression

---

query-expression

retrieves data or performs set operations on table-expressions.

Format

table-expression <set-operator table-expression>...

   where set-operator and the optional keywords are any of

<**INTERSECT** <CORRESPONDING> <ALL>>
<**OUTER UNION** <CORRESPONDING>>
<**UNION** <CORRESPONDING> <ALL>>
<**EXCEPT** <CORRESPONDING> <ALL>>

Description

A query-expression is composed of one or more table-expressions that can be linked optionally using set operators. A query-expression can be as simple as a short SELECT statement:

```
select * from table1;
```

Or, it can be as complex as several table-expressions linked with the UNION and EXCEPT operators. The primary purpose of a query-expression is to retrieve data from tables, PROC SQL views, and SAS/ACCESS views. They also help in creating tables and PROC SQL views and in inserting rows into a table; they can appear as in-line views or subqueries. See other component descriptions in this chapter for other uses of query-expressions.

The SQL procedure provides the traditional set operators from relational algebra: UNION, EXCEPT (difference), and INTERSECT. It also supports an OUTER UNION operator, which concatenates tables in a manner similar to the DATA step's SET statement.* Using set operators in query-expressions gives you more flexibility in merging tables and in handling complex queries.

A query-expression with set operators is evaluated as follows. Each table-expression is evaluated to produce an (internal) intermediate result table. Each intermediate result table then becomes an operand linked with a set operator to form an expression, for example, A UNION B. If the query-expression involves more than two table-expressions, the result from the first two becomes an operand for the next set operator and operand, for example, (A UNION B) EXCEPT C, ((A UNION B) EXCEPT C) INTERSECT D, and so on. Evaluating a query-expression produces a single output table that is displayed in the SAS OUTPUT window (during an interactive session) or sent to a list file (in batch mode).

The SQL procedure set operators follow this order of precedence unless it is overridden by parentheses in the expression(s):

INTERSECT	is evaluated first.
OUTER UNION, UNION, EXCEPT	have the same level of precedence.

The SQL procedure allows you to perform set operations even if the tables referred to in the table-expressions do not have the same number of columns. (The ANSI Standard for SQL requires that tables involved in a set operation have the same number of columns and that the columns have matching data types.) If a set operation is performed on a table that has fewer columns than the one(s) with which it is being linked, the SQL procedure extends the table with fewer columns by creating temporary (or virtual) columns with missing values of the appropriate data type. This temporary alteration enables the set

---

* For simplicity, *table* is used in the rest of this description to mean *table, PROC SQL view,* or *SAS/ACCESS view.*

operation to be performed correctly. In this example, a UNION operation is performed on a table with three columns and another with two columns.

```
data table1;
   input x y $ z;
   cards;
1 aaa 2
2 bbb 4
;

data table2;
   input x y $;
   cards;
5 ccc
6 ddd
;

proc sql;
select * from table1
union
select * from table2;
```

PROC SQL creates an internal, temporary table that extends Table2 with NULL or missing values. This temporary table consumes no disk space and does not require enough memory to store the entire table.

```
  X  Y         Z                    X  Y      Virtual Z
 ---------------- ---       union   ----------------------
     1  aaa      2                    5  ccc         .
     2  bbb      4                    6  ddd         .
```

Therefore, the union of Table1 and Table2 produces this result table:

```
                                                                    1
                  X  Y             Z
                 ----------------------------
                     1  aaa         2
                     2  bbb         4
                     5  ccc         .
                     6  ddd         .
```

Optional keywords   The optional CORRESPONDING keyword is used only when an optional set operator is also specified. CORRESPONDING can be abbreviated to CORR. CORRESPONDING causes the SQL procedure to match the columns in table-expressions *by name* and not by ordinal position. Columns that do not match by name are excluded from the result table, except for the OUTER UNION operator; see "OUTER UNION" later in this section.

For example, when performing a UNION on two table-expressions, the SQL procedure matches the first specified column-name (listed in the SELECT clause) from one table-expression with the first specified column-name from the other. Traditional systems based on SQL match the columns of a table only by ordinal position. If the CORRESPONDING keyword is omitted, the SQL procedure matches the columns in a table-expression by ordinal position.

The set operators automatically eliminate duplicate rows from their output tables. The optional ALL keyword leaves in the duplicate rows, reduces the processing by one step, and thereby improves a query-expression's performance. You use it when you want to display all the rows resulting from the table-expressions, rather than just the rows that are output because duplicates have been deleted. The ALL keyword is used only when an optional set operator is also specified. The ALL keyword is explained for each set operator in the examples that follow.

Examples

Each set operator is described and used in an example based on the following two tables created with DATA steps. Both the Lefty and Rightz tables have two columns: X is a numeric variable and is in both tables as the first column; Y is a character variable in Lefty, and Z is a character variable in Rightz.

```
data sql.lefty;
   input x y $;
   cards;
1 one
2 two
2 two
3 three
;

proc sql;
title 'Lefty Table';
select * from sql.lefty;
```

```
                         Lefty Table                           1
                            X  Y
                     ------------------
                            1  one
                            2  two
                            2  two
                            3  three
```

```
data sql.rightz;
   input x z $;
   cards;
1 one
2 two
4 four
;

proc sql;
title 'Rightz Table';
select * from sql.rightz;
```

```
                        Rightz Table                        1

                          X  Z
                        ------------------
                          1  one
                          2  two
                          4  four
```

OUTER UNION Performing an OUTER UNION is very similar to performing the SAS DATA step with a SET statement. The OUTER UNION concatenates the intermediate results from the table-expressions. Thus the result table for the query-expression contains all the rows produced by the first table-expression followed by all the rows produced by the second table-expression. Notice that columns with the same name are in separate columns in the result table.

```
proc sql;
select * from sql.lefty
outer union
select * from sql.rightz;
```

```
                                                            1

                  X  Y              X  Z
                ----------------------------------------
                  1  one            .
                  2  two            .
                  2  two            .
                  3  three          .
                  .                 1  one
                  .                 2  two
                  .                 4  four
```

When you use the OUTER UNION CORRESPONDING operator, the nonmatching columns are retained in the result table. For columns with the same name, if a value is missing from the result of the first table-expression, the value in that column from the second table-expression is inserted. Thus, in the following example, the X columns from the two table-expressions are concatenated:

```
proc sql;
select * from sql.lefty
outer union corresponding
select * from sql.rightz;
```

```
                                                            1

                  X  Y         Z
                ----------------------------
                  1  one
                  2  two
                  2  two
                  3  three
                  1            one
                  2            two
                  4            four
```

```
select * from sql.lefty
union corr
select * from sql.rightz;
```

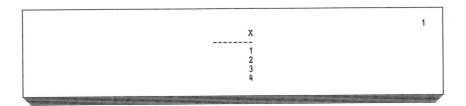

Notice that the output of this query has one column X, which is the only column that is common to the results of both table-expressions. The ALL keyword is not used with OUTER UNION because this operator's default action is to include all rows in a result table.

UNION   The UNION operator produces an output table that contains all the unique rows that result from both table-expressions. That is, the output table contains rows produced by the first table-expression, the second table-expression, or both.

The names of the columns in the output table are the names of the columns from the first table-expression unless a column (such as an expression) has no name in the first table-expression. In this case, the name of that column in the output table will be the name of the respective column in the second table-expression. The columns in the table-expressions must have compatible data types if CORRESPONDING is not specified.

```
proc sql;
select * from sql.lefty
union
select * from sql.rightz;
```

```
                              X  Y                        1
                          --------------------
                              1  one
                              2  two
                              3  three
                              4  four
```

The ALL keyword can be used to request that duplicate rows remain in the output table. This form of the query-expression evaluates more efficiently, as described earlier in "Optional keywords." The ALL keyword should be used when it does not matter if duplicate rows appear in the output.

```
select * from sql.lefty
union all
select * from sql.rightz;
```

```
                                                               1
                            X  Y
                           ------------------
                            1  one
                            2  two
                            2  two
                            3  three
                            1  one
                            2  two
                            4  four
```

EXCEPT   The EXCEPT operator produces an output table that has rows resulting from the first table-expression that are not the result of the second table-expression. EXCEPT is a set difference operator: if the intermediate result from the first table-expression has at least one occurrence of a row that is not in the intermediate result of the second table-expression, that row (from the first table-expression) is included in the result table.

The ALL keyword can be used to achieve slightly different results. In this case, the number of rows having some value X in the output table is the number of rows that have that value X resulting from the first table-expression minus the number of rows that have that same value X resulting from the second table-expression. If the second table-expression produces the same number of instances, or more instances, of row X, its result will not appear in the output table.

For example, if ten sailors were produced by the first table-expression and seven sailors by the second, the output table would have three sailors. The output of an EXCEPT ALL operation contains the rows produced by the first table-expression that cannot be matched one-to-one with a row produced by the second table-expression.

```
proc sql;
select * from sql.lefty
except all
select * from sql.rightz;
```

```
                                                               1
                            X  Y
                           ------------------
                            2  two
                            3  three
```

INTERSECT   The INTERSECT operator produces an output table having rows that belong to or are common to both tables.

The ALL keyword can be used to achieve slightly different results. In this case, the number of rows having some value X in the output table is the number of rows that produced that value X in both table-expressions.

For example, if ten sailors were produced by the first table-expression and seven sailors were produced by the second table-expression, the output table would have seven sailors. The output of an INTERSECT ALL operation contains the rows produced by the first table-expression that are matched one-to-one with a row produced by the second table-expression.

```
proc sql;
select * from sql.lefty
intersect
select * from sql.rightz;
```

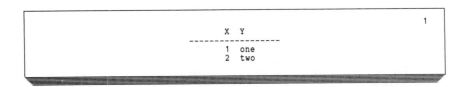

See Also
table-expression

---

set-clause

sets or resets data values in a row.

Format

SET column-name=sql-expression <, column-name=sql-expression>...

Description
The SET clause is used in the INSERT and UPDATE statements to set or alter the value of a column in a table or SAS/ACCESS view. See "INSERT Statement" and "UPDATE Statement" for more information on using the SET clause with these statements. The SET keyword is repeated for each row of a table or SAS/ACCESS view; the SET clauses are not separated by commas.

In the SET clause, a column reference on the left side of the equals sign can also appear as part of the sql-expression on the right side of the sign. That is, it is possible to modify a column in terms of itself, for example, to mark down the price of merchandise for an end-of-the-summer sale:

```
set prodlist=prodlist*.25
```

Examples

This example creates a table and uses the SAS function UPCASE to set the query results in uppercase.

```
proc sql;
create table sql.xyzzy as
    select empnum, empname, empyears
        from sql.employee
        where emptitle='manager';

select * from sql.xyzzy;
```

```
                                                                         1
                    EMPNUM  EMPNAME   EMPYEARS
                    ----------------------------
                       201  Betty            8
                       301  Sally            9
                       401  Chuck           12
```

```
update sql.xyzzy
    set empname=upcase(empname), empyears=20;

select * from sql.xyzzy;
```

```
                                                                         1
                    EMPNUM  EMPNAME   EMPYEARS
                    ----------------------------
                       201  BETTY           20
                       301  SALLY           20
                       401  CHUCK           20
```

See Also

INSERT statement, UPDATE statement

sql-expression

lists operands that can be used in functions and expressions and the operators that connect them.

Format

The operands of the sql-expression are listed here. The operators that connect the operands are described later in this section. Each of the following is a valid operand in an sql-expression:

constant
column-name
SAS-function
summary-function
<ALL | ANY> (query-expression)
USER

Description

An sql-expression is a sequence of operands and operators that produces a result value. The operands are column names, functions, and constants; "Format" lists the types of operands available in the SQL procedure. The operators are special-character operators, functions, and grouping parentheses and are described later in this section. There are operators for most mathematical expressions (for example, +), as well as many others for manipulating both numeric and character data. Expressions in the SQL procedure follow the same rules as expressions in the SAS DATA step and in many other programming languages. See *SAS Language: Reference* for more information on expressions.

A *constant* is a number or a character string in quotes (or other special notation) that indicates a fixed value. Constants are also called *literals*. Constants are described in Chapter 4, "Rules of the SAS Language," in *SAS Language: Reference*.

The SQL procedure supports the same SAS functions as the DATA step, except for the special functions LAG, DIF, and SOUND. See Chapter 11, "SAS Functions," in *SAS Language: Reference* for more information. Summary functions are also SAS functions. See "summary-function" later in this chapter for more information.

The SQL procedure also supports the ANSI SQL function COALESCE. The COALESCE function accepts a varying number of arguments, which must all be of the same data type. The COALESCE function returns the first argument whose value is not a SAS missing value. In some SQL databases, the COALESCE function is called the IFNULL function. See Appendix 2 for more information on the ANSI Standard for SQL.

For example, in COALESCE(V1,V2), if V1 is a missing value but V2 has a value, the function returns V2's value as its result and V1 is left unchanged. If V1 has a value, its value is returned. This latter statement can also be written with a case-expression.

```
case when v1 is not null then v1 else v2 end;
```

See "Complex Joins" in Chapter 3 for another example of the COALESCE function.

Query-expressions are called *subqueries* in this context and are described later in this description in "Subqueries".

USER is a literal that references the userid of the person who submitted the program. The userid returned is host-system-dependent, but the SQL procedure uses the same value that the &SYSJOBID macro variable has on the system. USER can be specified in a view definition, for example, to create a view that restricts access to those people in the USER's department:

```
create view myemp as
   select * from dept12.employees
      where manager=user;
```

This view produces a different set of employee information for each manager who references it. That is, if manager Martin McClelland runs this statement under his userid, he will get different information than manager Julia Storm gets when she runs it under her userid.

Operators and the Order of Evaluation

The order in which operations are evaluated is the same as in the DATA step with this one exception: NOT is grouped with the logical operators AND and OR in the SQL procedure; in the DATA step, NOT is grouped with the unary plus and minus signs.

Unlike some versions of SQL, missing values in the SAS System always come first in the collating sequence. Therefore, in Boolean and comparison operations, the following expressions evaluate to true in a predicate:

```
 3>null
-3>null
 0>null
```

You can use parentheses to group values or to nest mathematical expressions. Parentheses make expressions easier to read and can also be used to change the order of evaluation of the operators. Evaluating expressions with parentheses begins at the deepest level of parentheses and moves outward. For example, the base SAS software evaluates A+B*C as A+(B*C), though you could add parentheses to make it evaluate as (A+B)*C for a different result.

Higher priority operations are performed first: that is, group 0 operators are evaluated before group 5 operators. Table 5.1 shows the SQL procedure's operators and order of evaluation, including their priority groups.

	Group	Operator	Description
Table 5.1 *Operators and Order of Evaluation*	0	( )	forces the expression enclosed to be evaluated first
	1	case-expression	
	2	**	raises to a power
		unary +, unary −	indicates a positive or negative number
		><	selects minimum of its operands
		<>	selects maximum of its operands
	3	*	multiplies
		/	divides
	4	+	adds
		−	subtracts
	5	||	concatenates
	6	<NOT> between-condition	
		<NOT> contains-condition	
		<NOT> exists-condition	
		<NOT> in-condition	
		is <NOT> condition	
		<NOT> like-condition	
	7	=	equals
		¬=	does not equal
		^=	
		>	is greater than
		<	is less than
		>=	is greater than or equal to
		<=	is less than or equal to
		=*	sounds like
	8	AND &	indicates logical AND
	9	OR |	indicates logical OR
	10	NOT ¬ or ^	indicates logical NOT

Notice that symbols for operators vary some, depending on the host system. For example, on microcomputers and minicomputers, the symbol for *not equal* is ^=. However, you can also use the operators **NOT=** or **NE** to symbolize *not equal*. See Chapter 4 in *SAS Language: Reference* for more information on operators and expressions.

The SQL procedure operator *sounds-like* (=*) is used only with character operands. The sounds-like operator selects rows based on a comparison of two expressions. It returns true if a spelling variant of the name sounds the same as the given name; that is, it displays names that match or sound like the left operand.

This operator is evaluated using the Soundex algorithm. The sounds-like operator is often used in airline reservation, phone directory, and genealogy applications to find names that are similar or have similar spellings. Take the following example, where the data set is created in a DATA step:

```
data sql.people;
   length fname $ 8 lname $ 16;
   input fname lname;
   cards;
Magnolia Lewis
Joe Louis
David Johnson
Tom Johnsson
Susan Johnston
Matthew Johnsen
Larry Jiles
Aretha Giles
John Geil
Ione Gin
;

proc sql;
select * from sql.people where lname=*"Johnson" order by 2;
```

```
                                                            1
     FNAME      LNAME
     --------------------------
     Matthew    Johnsen
     David      Johnson
     Tom        Johnsson
```

```
select * from sql.people where lname=*"Lewis";
```

```
                                                            1
     FNAME      LNAME
     --------------------------
     Magnolia   Lewis
     Joe        Louis
```

In this last example, the algorithm finds only the names listed and none of the others with the similar spellings and sounds, for instance, Geil and Jiles. While the sounds-like operator is often useful, it is not failsafe.

```
select * from sql.people
    where (lname=*"Gin") or (lname=*"Giles");
```

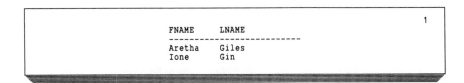

```
                                                                      1
          FNAME     LNAME
          ---------------------------
          Aretha    Giles
          Ione      Gin
```

The SQL procedure operator CONTAINS is used only with character operands. The CONTAINS operator returns true and displays rows if the right-hand expression is a subsequence or part of the left-hand expression, as in this example:

```
select distinct * from sql.customer
    where custcity contains 'Beach';
```

```
                                                                      1
          CUSTNAME     CUSTNUM  CUSTCITY
          ------------------------------------
          Coast Shop         3  Myrtle Beach
          Coast Shop         5  Myrtle Beach
          Coast Shop        12  Virginia Beach
          Del Mar            3  Folly Beach
          New Waves          6  Virginia Beach
          Sea Sports        20  Virginia Beach
```

Subqueries

A subquery is a query-expression that is nested as part of another query-expression. Depending on the clause that contains it, a subquery can return a single value or multiple values. If more than one subquery is used in a query-expression, the innermost query is evaluated first, then the next innermost query, and so on, moving outward in the levels of nesting.

The SQL procedure allows a subquery (contained in parentheses) at any point in an expression where a simple column value or constant can be used. In this case, a subquery must return a *single value*, that is, one row with only one column. When a subquery returns one value, you can name the value with a column alias and refer to it by that name elsewhere in the query.

When a subquery returns only one value, it is possible to compare a column value to the result of a subquery. For example, "Who lives in the same city as Herb?" can be answered if you determine first the city in which Herb lives and then compare that value with the cities in which other employees live.

```
proc sql;
title 'Who Lives Near Herb?';
select empname
    from sql.employee
    where empcity=(select empcity
                     from sql.employee
                     where empname='Herb');
```

The subquery returns the value `Ocean City`. This value is then used as if it were a literal in the WHERE expression or, as if the expression were written as follows:

```
where empcity='Ocean City';
```

```
                          Who Lives Near Herb?                          1

                          EMPNAME
                          --------
                          Herb
                          Betty
                          Wanda
                          Fred
```

Subqueries that are included with the IN clause or EXISTS condition can return *multiple values*. In this example, a sales representative's name and his or her manager's name are listed for each sales representative who has made a sale.

```
select e1.empnum, e1.empname, e2.empname as manager
    from sql.employee as e1,
         sql.employee as e2
    where e1.empboss=e2.empnum and
          e1.empnum in
             (select empnum from sql.invoice)
    order by 2;
```

```
                                                                        1
              EMPNUM  EMPNAME  MANAGER
              -------------------------
                 216  Fred     Betty
                 213  Joe      Betty
                 314  Marvin   Sally
                 318  Nick     Sally
                 417  Sam      Chuck
                 215  Wanda    Betty
```

In the previous example, the Employee table is joined with itself. The subquery returns all the rows with employee numbers (EMPNUM) in the Invoice table; they are defined as a set because of the IN condition. The WHERE expression then selects rows where the boss's numbers in Employee table 1 (E1) are matched with the employee numbers in Employee table 2 (E2) and where the employee numbers in Employee table 1 are members of the set of values defined in the subquery.

Sometimes it is helpful to compare a value with a set of values returned by a subquery. The keywords ANY or ALL can be specified before a subquery when the subquery is the right-hand operand of a comparison. If ALL is specified, the comparison is true only if it is true for all values returned by the subquery. If a subquery returns no rows, the result of an ALL comparison is true.

```
title 'Who Has Worked Here Longer Than Any Single Salesrep?';
select empname
   from sql.employee
   where empyears>all (select empyears
                          from sql.employee
                          where emptitle='salesrep');
```

```
          Who Has Worked Here Longer Than Any Single Salesrep?              1

                              EMPNAME
                              --------
                              Herb
                              Chuck
```

This subquery follows the ALL keyword and returns the number of years that each sales representative has worked into the right operand. These numbers are compared with the years that all employees have worked (in the left operand). The comparison is true because **Herb**, the president, and **Chuck**, a manager, have worked at the wholesale company longer than all the sales representatives.

If ANY is specified, the comparison is true if it is true for any one of the values returned by the subquery. If a subquery returns no rows, the result of an ANY comparison is false.

```
title 'Do Any Salesreps Have More Service Than a Manager?';
select empname
   from sql.employee
   where emptitle='salesrep'
        and empyears>any (select empyears
                             from sql.employee
                             where emptitle='manager');
```

```
          Do Any Salesreps Have More Service Than a Manager?              1
                              EMPNAME
                              --------
                              Wanda
```

Here the ANY comparison returned one true value, **Wanda**, so the entire comparison is evaluated as true.

Correlated subqueries   In a correlated subquery, the values returned by the subquery depend on values in the current row of an outer query. That is, the WHERE expression in a subquery refers to values in a table in the outer query. For example, the WHERE expression in this subquery must refer to rows in the Invoice table in the outer query in order to evaluate the subquery. This query lists products sold to stores in `Myrtle Beach` .

```
proc sql;
select distinct prodname
   from sql.invoice as i
   where 'Myrtle Beach' in
      (select distinct custcity
          from sql.customer as c
          where c.custname=i.custname and
                c.custnum=i.custnum);
```

```
                                                             1

                   PRODNAME
                   ----------
                   windsurfer
                   raft
                   snorkel
                   flippers
```

The correlated subquery is evaluated for each row in the outer query. Look, for example, at the first row of the Invoice table (outer query) and the first row of the Customer table (subquery). The subquery matches the customer name and number values, `Beach Land` and 16, from the first row of the Invoice table with the values in the Customer table. Thus, for this row, the subquery effectively becomes

```
(select distinct custcity
   from sql.customer as c
   where c.custname='Beach Land' and
         c.custnum=16);
```

The subquery is executed, building an internal table that contains the customer city `Ocean City`. For this row, the original query then becomes

```
proc sql;
select distinct prodname
   from sql.invoice as i
   where 'Myrtle Beach' in ('Ocean City');
```

The condition in the WHERE expression is not satisfied (that is, it is false), so the first row of the Invoice table is not selected for the result table. The subquery evaluates for each row in the outer query until all the rows that satisfy the WHERE expression are selected and displayed.

See Also
column-name, host-variable, query-expression, summary-function

summary-function

performs statistical calculations.

Format

summary-function (<DISTINCT | ALL > sql-expression)

Description

Summary functions produce a statistical summary of the entire table listed in the FROM clause or for each group specified in a GROUP BY clause.* These functions reduce all the values in each row or column in a table to one *summarizing* or *aggregate* value. For this reason, these functions are often called *aggregate functions*. For example, the sum (one value) of a row results from the addition of all the values in the row; the values in each row of the table are added in this way. Or for the MAX function, the SAS System determines the maximum value in a column by considering all the values in that column and selecting the highest one; the values in each column of the table are evaluated likewise.

A summary function's value for a particular group is determined based on the data associated with that group. Groups are specified with a GROUP BY clause; if this clause is omitted, all the rows in the table are considered to be a single group. See "group-by-item" earlier in this chapter for information on the GROUP BY clause and summary functions.

The SQL procedure can process the following statistics; notice that some functions have more than one name to accomodate both SAS and SQL conventions:

AVG, MEAN	means or average of values
COUNT, FREQ, N	number of nonmissing values
CSS	corrected sum of squares
CV	coefficient of variation (percent)
MAX	largest value
MIN	smallest value
NMISS	number of missing values
PRT	probability of a greater absolute value of Student's *t*
RANGE	range of values
STD	standard deviation
STDERR	standard error of the mean
SUM	sum of values

---

* For simplicity, *table* is used in this description to mean *table*, *PROC SQL view*, or *SAS/ACCESS view*.

SUMWGT	sum of the WEIGHT variable values*
T	Student's *t* value for testing the hypothesis that the population mean is zero
USS	uncorrected sum of squares
VAR	variance.

For a description and the formulas used for these statistics, refer to "SAS Elementary Statistics Procedures" in the *SAS Procedures Guide*.

The optional SQL keyword DISTINCT causes the SQL procedure to calculate the statistic based on the distinct (that is, nonduplicating) values of the sql-expression. For example, if the name `Paul` were in the Sailors table more than once, the following statement calculates the number of sailors but counts duplicate names (such as `Paul`) only once.

```
select count(distinct name) from sailors;
```

A summary function cannot appear in the ON clause described earlier in "joined-table." A summary function also cannot appear in a WHERE expression unless that expression contains a subquery and the summary function is in the SELECT or FROM clauses of that subquery. For example, the first of the next two clauses is a valid WHERE expression; the second is not:

```
where 20>(select sum(x) from t1)
where 20>max(x)
```

If the SELECT clause of a table-expression contains one or more summary functions and that table-expression evaluates to no rows, the summary function results are missing values, with the following exceptions, which return zeros:

COUNT(*)

COUNT(<DISTINCT> sql-expression)

NMISS(<DISTINCT> sql-expression)

Calculating statistics based on the number of arguments   The number of arguments specified in a summary function affects how the calculation is performed. If you specify a single argument, the values in the column are calculated; if you specify multiple arguments, the arguments or columns listed are calculated for each row. Take, for example, calculations on the following table:

```
data sql.summary;
   input x y z;
   cards;
1 2 3
4 5 6
7 8 9
;
```

---

*   Currently, there is no way to designate a WEIGHT variable for a table in the SQL procedure. Thus, each row (or observation) has a weight of 1.

```
proc sql;
title 'Summary Table';
select * from sql.summary;
```

```
                           Summary Table                         1
                    X          Y          Z
               ------------------------------
                    1          2          3
                    4          5          6
                    7          8          9
```

If you specify one argument (or column name) in the summary function, as in the following example, it calculates the statistic down the column. This process is comparable to the MEANS procedure, which computes statistics on columns of a table.

```
title 'Column-wise Summary Statistics';
select sum(x) as sum_x, min(y) as min_y, max(z) as max_z
   from sql.summary;
```

```
                  Column-wise Summary Statistics                 1
                    SUM_X      MIN_Y      MAX_Z
               ------------------------------
                     12          2          9
```

Here the SUM function adds all the values in column X; the MIN and MAX functions list the lowest and highest values in the Y and Z columns, respectively. Thus, the SUM function reduces all the values in a column to a single value by getting the values' sum or by displaying the lowest and highest values.

If you specify more than one argument (or column name) in a summary function, as in the following example, it calculates all the values listed in the function call. This action is comparable to that of the SUM function in the DATA step.

```
title 'Row-wise Summary Statistics';
select *, sum(x,y,z) as rowsum
   from sql.summary;
```

```
                    Row-wise Summary Statistics                  1
                X          Y          Z      ROWSUM
           ----------------------------------------
                1          2          3          6
                4          5          6         15
                7          8          9         24
```

Here the SUM function adds the values along each row and displays the result in the ROWSUM column. Again, the SUM function reduces the values in each row to one value.

If you use an arithmetic expression as the argument to a summary function, for example SUM($x+y$), the SQL procedure can evaluate it almost as quickly as it can evaluate a single column or argument, for example, SUM(x).

Evaluating summary functions with nonsummary expressions   A summary function can appear in a SELECT clause or a HAVING clause. When a summary function appears in either of these clauses along with one or more other arithmetic expressions or columns (that is, variables), the results from the summary function may have to be remerged into the original data.

It is necessary to remerge the data when a summary function's result value is involved in a calculation or is compared with columns that are not in the query-expression's optional GROUP BY clause. Remerging involves two passes through the data. The first pass calculates the summary function's values for each row, and the second one redistributes the result values across the rows (that is, original data) of the source table.

The SQL procedure remerges with the data if one of the following conditions is true:

□   The object-items listed in the SELECT clause contain a column-name that is not listed in the query's GROUP BY clause.

□   The object-items that appear in a HAVING clause that is associated with a SELECT clause (within the same table-expression) have one of the following conditions:

　　□   a column-name that is not included in a subquery and is not listed in the GROUP BY clause

　　□   a correlated reference that is not listed as a column-name in the GROUP BY clause.

In these conditions, notice that references are only to column-names used in the SELECT clause.

Take, for example, the case where you want to display the values of a column as well as the percentage that each value (row) contributes to the total (sum) of that column. This calculation requires two passes through the data: one pass to compute the sum total and the second pass to compute the percentage of the total for each value (or row) in the column.

The SQL procedure enables you to accomplish these two tasks in a single query. This example computes the percentage for each row of the column (that is, multiplies X by 100 and divides it by the sum of X) and compares them with the values in column X of the Summary table. Notice that because a GROUP BY clause has been omitted from this query, the values listed in the SELECT clause are handled as a single group. The note is written to the SAS log.

```
proc sql;
select x, (100*x/sum(x)) as p_total
   from sql.summary;


NOTE: The query requires remerging the summary statistics
      back with the original data.
```

```
                         X   P_TOTAL                              1
                      -------------------
                         1   8.333333
                         4  33.33333
                         7  58.33333
```

When the SQL procedure detects that the SELECT clause contains both a summary function (which returns a single, constant value) and other columns (in which each row of the group is different), it invokes a special logic called *remerging*. In such cases, the SQL procedure calculates and returns the value of the summary function first and then uses this result to calculate the arithmetic expressions in which the summary function participates. Thus, in the previous example, the sum of X is used to calculate the percentage.

Evaluating summary and nonsummary expressions in one query is a SAS System extension to SQL. The more common way of satisfying this request is to create a view that computes the total and then join that view with the original data, as shown here. The note is written to the SAS log.

```
create view totalx as
   select sum(x) as totx
      from sql.summary;

select x, (100*x/totx) as p_total
   from sql.summary, totalx;

NOTE: SQL view WORK.TOTALX defined.
```

```
                         X   P_TOTAL                              1
                      -------------------
                         1   8.333333
                         4  33.33333
                         7  58.33333
```

You can use the SQL procedure to accomplish this task with just one query. If you want to expand the calculations to handle other groups in a table, you can add a GROUP BY clause.

Examples

The following example lists the number of different customers for each product whose outstanding inventory count is more than 30 units:

```
proc sql;
select prodname as products,
       count(distinct custname) label='Number of Customers'
   from sql.invoice as i1
   group by prodname
   having (select sum(invqty)
              from sql.invoice
              where prodname=i1.prodname)>30
   order by 1,2;
```

```
                                 Number of                           1
                      PRODUCTS   Customers
                      ---------------------
                      flippers       5
                      raft           4
                      snorkel        5
```

Notice that no remerging occurs because PRODNAME appears in the GROUP BY clause.

This example shows the total sales to each customer and the fraction of the total sales for which the customer is responsible. The note is written to the SAS log.

```
select custname, sales,
         100*sales/sum(sales) as contrib format=6.2
    from (select custname, sum(invqty*invprice) as sales
             from sql.invoice
             group by custname);

NOTE: The query reqires remerging the summary statistics
      back with the original data.
```

```
                                                                    1
                  CUSTNAME     SALES  CONTRIB
                  ---------------------------
                  Beach Land     705     4.24
                  Coast Shop    4935    29.71
                  Del Mar       2105    12.67
                  New Waves     3615    21.76
                  Surf Mart     5250    31.61
```

In this example, the in-line view returns the total sales per customer and the outer query compares each customer's contribution to the total sale for that customer. The GROUP BY clause is within the in-line view and references CUSTNAME in that view, not the CUSTNAME of the outer query, so that the results of the outer query are remerged with the original data.

See Also

group-by-item, having-expression, object-item, sql-expression, table-expression

---

table-expression

defines a query's result table.

Format

SELECT <**DISTINCT**> object-item <, object-item>...	SELECT clause
<**INTO** host-variable <, host-variable>... >	INTO clause
FROM from-list	FROM clause
<where-expression>	WHERE clause
<**GROUP BY** group-by-item <, group-by-item>... >	GROUP BY clause
<having-expression>	HAVING clause

Description

A table-expression is the fundamental building block of most SQL procedure statements. It identifies the form of the result table that you want. All of the components in a table-expression are described in detail elsewhere in this chapter.

Table-expressions, combined optionally with set operators (UNION, OUTER UNION, EXCEPT, and INTERSECT), make up a query-expression. Query-expressions can also appear in FROM clauses as in-line views and in WHERE and HAVING clauses as subqueries. Most query-expressions do not involve set operators and are just single table-expressions, each ending with a semicolon.

The DISTINCT keyword causes the SQL procedure to eliminate duplicate rows from the result table. For example, if a query would return four rows for each instance of the **Surf Mart** store, specifying DISTINCT omits the duplicate rows and returns one row for **Surf Mart**.

Examples

Table-expressions can be combined using the set operators to make one query-expression. In this example, two table expressions are linked using the set operator INTERSECT. This query displays products that were sold in Myrtle Beach by employees who live in Virginia Beach:

```
proc sql;
   select distinct prodname
      from sql.customer as c, sql.invoice as i
      where c.custname=i.custname and
            c.custnum=i.custnum and
            c.custcity='Myrtle Beach'
   intersect
   select distinct prodname
      from sql.invoice as i, sql.employee as e
      where e.empnum=i.empnum and
      e.empcity='Virginia Beach';
```

```
                                                                        1
                        PRODNAME
                        ----------
                        raft
                        snorkel
```

If the first table-expression were executed alone as a SELECT statement (ending with a semicolon), it would return all the products sold in Myrtle Beach: **windsurfer, raft, flippers, snorkel**. Likewise, if the second table-expression were executed alone as a SELECT statement, it would return the products sold by employees living in Virginia Beach: **raft, surfboard, snorkel**. When both table-expressions are combined into a query-expression containing the INTERSECT operator, the products are displayed that each table-expression result has in common, that is, **raft** and **snorkel**.

The last query displays the job titles listed in the Employee table. The DISTINCT keyword eliminates rows with duplicate titles and the ORDER BY clause sorts and displays the rows to be displayed in alphabetical order.

```
select distinct emptitle
   from sql.employee
   order by emptitle;
```

```
                                                                        1
                        EMPTITLE
                        ----------
                        manager
                        president
                        salesrep
```

See Also
from-list, group-by-item, having-expression, host-variable, object-item, query-expression, sql-expression, where-expression

table-name

defines the valid forms of a table name.

Format

<libref.>table <(dataset-option <dataset-option>...)>

Description
A table (or SAS data file) can be specified in almost every SQL procedure statement. A table is referred to by its name in most statements or by an optional alias in a query-expression's FROM clause; see "from-list" earlier in this chapter for information on table aliases.

SAS data set options can be applied to table names whenever tables are referred to or created. You can specify these options (separated with spaces) by enclosing them in parentheses immediately following the table name. For more information, see "SQL Procedure and SAS Data Set Options" earlier in this chapter and the options' descriptions in *SAS Language: Reference*.

Librefs and storing tables   In the SAS System, a data set's complete name has two levels, for example SQL.PRODUCT. The SQL procedure can refer to one or both of these names. The first-level name is a *libref* (short for SAS data library reference) and indicates where a SAS data library is stored. The second-level name identifies the specific table in the data library.

A SAS data library must exist—and a libref be assigned to it—before you can create a table that is to be stored in that data library. You specify a libref when you create a permanently stored table, unless you use the SAS data set option USER= in the CREATE statement. You must also use the two-level name when referring to a table in the FROM clause of a query.

When a second-level name is used alone, it usually refers to a temporarily stored table, except in the case of SQL views; see "CREATE Statement" earlier in this chapter for more information. If a table is temporarily stored, a libref is optional. If the libref is omitted, the table is assumed to be a member of the temporary SAS data library WORK.

See *SAS Language: Reference* for more information on creating SAS data libraries, librefs, and storing SAS data sets.

Examples

This example creates and displays data using the Nosales table. Since no libref is specified in the CREATE statement, the Nosales table is stored temporarily in the default SAS data library WORK; it will be erased when the SAS batch job or interactive session ends. The result table displays customers who did not buy their products from the sample wholesale company. The note is written to the SAS log.

```
create table nosales as
   select distinct custname
      from sql.customer
      where custname not in
            (select custname from sql.invoice)
   order by custname;

select * from nosales;

NOTE:  Table WORK.NOSALES created, with 1 column and 1 row.
```

The newly created table is not displayed in SAS output unless you perform a query on it. In this case, a query is executed and the Nosales table is displayed.

```
                                                            1
               CUSTNAME
               ----------
               Sea Sports
```

If you had created Nosales as a permanent table, you could refer to it later in queries and statements during other SAS jobs or sessions.

The last example creates a temporary view that displays the sales representatives by the number of sales (number of invoices) they have made.

Here, two tables are joined to produce the Salenum view, and each table takes an alias in the FROM clause.

```
create view salenum as
   select name, count(*) as numinv
      from sql.employee(rename=(empname=name)) as e,
           sql.invoice as i
      where e.empnum=i.empnum
      group by name
      order by numinv;

select * from salenum;
```

```
                                                                      1
              NAME      NUMINV
              ------------------
              Marvin        2
              Fred          2
              Wanda         3
              Joe           4
              Nick          9
              Sam          10
```

The SAS data set option RENAME= changes the column named EMPNAME to NAME in the Employee table, which is reflected in the view's output. Notice that the RENAME= option is associated with the Employee table, which underlies the view; you can only associate data set options with the view's source table(s), not with the view name itself.

See Also
CREATE statement, from-list

---

values-clause

specifies values in a row.

Format

VALUES (*value* <, *value*>...)
<**VALUES** (*value* <, *value*>...)>...

Description
The VALUES clause is used in the INSERT statement to specify the values in the rows to be inserted. One row is inserted for each VALUES clause. The order of the values must match the order of the column names in the INSERT column list or, if no list is specified, the order of the columns in the table or SAS/ACCESS view. The values in the row must match the data type of their respective columns.

Example

This example creates a small table and adds values by means of the VALUES clause. Notice that a comma does not separate the two VALUES clauses. The notes are written to the SAS log.

```
proc sql;
create table valtest (x numeric, y numeric, z char);

insert into valtest
   values(1,2,'happy')
   values(3,4,'sad');

select * from valtest;

NOTE: Table WORK.VALTEST created, with 0 rows and 3 columns.
NOTE: 2 rows were inserted in table WORK.VALEST.
```

```
                                                                  1
                        X         Y   Z
              -----------------------------
                        1         2   happy
                        3         4   sad
```

See Also

INSERT statement

---

where-expression

tests for values that satisfy specified conditions and displays rows in a result table based on them.

Format

WHERE sql-expression

Description

The WHERE expression is one of the optional clauses in a table-expression. In the SQL procedure, the WHERE expression is any valid sql-expression (with one qualification noted later). An sql-expression consists of one or more conditions or *predicates* that are evaluated as Boolean (true/false) expressions. Each predicate sets certain criteria for including a row from a source table in the result table. *
When a condition is met (that is, the condition evaluates to true), those rows are displayed in the result table; otherwise, no rows are displayed.

A summary function is one of the predicates that can be included in an sql-expression, but a WHERE expression cannot contain a summary function unless it is part of a subquery. That is, a WHERE expression can contain a

---

* For simplicity, *table* is used in this description to mean *table, PROC SQL view,* or *SAS/ACCESS view.*

subquery and a summary function can appear in the SELECT or FROM clauses of that subquery, as shown in the first of the following two examples:

```
where 20>(select sum(x) from t1)    /*  valid WHERE expression   */
where 20>sum(x)                      /*  invalid WHERE expression */
```

Example

This example lists the dollar amount for sales made where the customer and sales representative lived in the same city. Notice the use of both comparison and logical operators in the WHERE expression; see "sql-expression" earlier in this chapter for more information on operators and their order of evaluation.

```
proc sql;
select invnum, custname, custnum, empnum,
       (invqty*invprice) as sales
   from sql.invoice
   where (select distinct empcity
            from sql.employee
            where empnum=invoice.empnum)
         =
         (select distinct custcity
            from sql.customer
            where custname=invoice.custname and
                  custnum=invoice.custnum)
   order by 1;
```

```
                                                                          1
        INVNUM  CUSTNAME    CUSTNUM    EMPNUM    SALES
        -------------------------------------------------
           280  Beach Land      16       215      280
           290  Beach Land      16       216      285
           300  Beach Land      16       216      140
           310  Coast Shop       3       318     2610
           320  Coast Shop       3       318      180
           330  Coast Shop       5       318       75
           340  Coast Shop       5       318      285
           350  Coast Shop       5       318      240
           360  Coast Shop       5       318      150
           370  Coast Shop      12       213       70
           380  Coast Shop      14       417     1325
           410  Del Mar          8       417      240
           420  Del Mar         11       417      105
           430  Del Mar         11       417      150
           440  Del Mar         11       417      380
           450  New Waves        3       215      100
           460  New Waves        3       215      200
           470  New Waves        6       213      225
           480  New Waves        6       213     2940
           490  New Waves        6       213      150
           500  Surf Mart      101       417      280
           510  Surf Mart      101       417     1480
           520  Surf Mart      101       417      180
```

See Also

sql-expression, table-expression

Chapter Summary

This chapter has described the SQL procedure statements, options, and the components that make up those statements. It serves as a reference guide for the entire book. For more information and examples on using the statements and components, see Chapters 1 through 4.

Part 4
Appendices

Appendix 1   **Sample Tables**

Appendix 2   **SQL Procedure and the ANSI Standard for SQL˜**

184

Appendix **1** Sample Tables

Introduction 185

Employee Table 185

Customer Table 186

Product Table 187

Invoice Table 187

Introduction

This appendix describes and displays the four permanent tables used in most of the examples in this book. These tables represent sales information for a fictional beach-supplies wholesale company. Tables that have been created and used in one statement or component description are not repeated here because they apply only to that one example.

A SAS program to create these tables can be found in the member SQLUGDAT of the SAS System Sample Library. There are other members in this sample library (pointed to with the libref SQL) that demonstrate features of the SQL procedure.

Employee Table

The Employee table lists employees of the wholesale company. Each row in the table is uniquely identified by an employee number. Sales representatives report to managers, who report to the president. This chain of command is indicated in the EMPBOSS column. The columns are

EMPNUM	employee number
EMPNAME	employee name
EMPYEARS	years of service
EMPCITY	city in which employee lives
EMPTITLE	job title
EMPBOSS	employee number of employee's supervisor.

The following SELECT statement displays the Employee table:

```
proc sql;
title 'Employee Table';
select * from sql.employee;
```

```
                              Employee Table                          1

        EMPNUM  EMPNAME  EMPYEARS  EMPCITY            EMPTITLE    EMPBOSS
        ---------------------------------------------------------------
           101  Herb          28  Ocean City         president        .
           201  Betty          8  Ocean City         manager        101
           213  Joe            2  Virginia Beach     salesrep       201
           214  Jeff           1  Virginia Beach     salesrep       201
           215  Wanda         10  Ocean City         salesrep       201
           216  Fred           6  Ocean City         salesrep       201
           301  Sally          9  Wilmington         manager        101
           314  Marvin         5  Wilmington         salesrep       301
           318  Nick           1  Myrtle Beach       salesrep       301
           401  Chuck         12  Charleston         manager        101
           417  Sam            7  Charleston         salesrep       401
```

Customer Table

The Customer table describes each store that is an actual or potential purchaser of the wholesale company's products. Each table row is uniquely identified by a combination of a customer name and number. The columns are

CUSTNAME   name of customer company

CUSTNUM   customer number that identifies a particular store

CUSTCITY   city in which store is located.

The following SELECT statement displays the Customer table:

```
title 'Customer Table';
select * from sql.customer;
```

```
                         Customer Table                    1

            CUSTNAME     CUSTNUM  CUSTCITY
            ------------------------------------
            Beach Land        16  Ocean City
            Coast Shop         3  Myrtle Beach
            Coast Shop         5  Myrtle Beach
            Coast Shop        12  Virginia Beach
            Coast Shop        14  Charleston
            Del Mar            3  Folly Beach
            Del Mar            8  Charleston
            Del Mar           11  Charleston
            New Waves          3  Ocean City
            New Waves          6  Virginia Beach
            Sea Sports         8  Charleston
            Sea Sports        20  Virginia Beach
            Surf Mart        101  Charleston
            Surf Mart        118  Surfside
            Surf Mart        127  Ocean Isle
            Surf Mart        133  Charleston
```

Product Table

The Product table describes products that the wholesale company offers for sale. Each table row is uniquely identified by a product name. The columns are

PRODNAME   product name

PRODCOST   unit cost paid by wholesale company

PRODLIST   suggested list price paid by customer.

The following SELECT statement displays the Product table:

```
title 'Product Table';
select * from sql.product;
```

```
                        Product Table                          1

              PRODNAME   PRODCOST  PRODLIST
              -----------------------------
              flippers        $16       $20
              jet ski     $2,150    $2,675
              kayak          $190      $240
              raft             $5        $7
              snorkel         $12       $15
              surfboard      $615      $750
              windsurfer   $1,090    $1,325
```

Invoice Table

The Invoice table describes product sales made by sales representatives to customer stores. Each table row is uniquely identified by an invoice number. Some columns of the Invoice table refer to columns in the other three tables. The EMPNUM column in the Invoice table refers to the EMPNUM column in the Employee table. PRODNAME refers to the Product table. CUSTNAME and CUSTNUM refer to the Customer table. The columns are

INVNUM   invoice number

CUSTNAME   name of customer company

CUSTNUM   customer number that identifies a particular store

EMPNUM   sales representative's employee number

PRODNAME   product name

INVQTY   invoice quantity--number of units sold

INVPRICE   invoice unit price negotiated at time of sale.

The following SELECT statement displays the Invoice table:

```
title 'Invoice Table';
select * from sql.invoice;
```

```
                        Invoice Table                          1

  INVNUM  CUSTNAME    CUSTNUM    EMPNUM  PRODNAME    INVQTY  INVPRICE
  ------------------------------------------------------------------
     280  Beach Land       16       215  snorkel         20       $14
     290  Beach Land       16       216  flippers        15       $19
     300  Beach Land       16       216  raft            20        $7
     310  Coast Shop        3       318  windsurfer       2    $1,305
     320  Coast Shop        3       318  raft            30        $6
     330  Coast Shop        5       318  snorkel          5       $15
     340  Coast Shop        5       318  flippers        15       $19
     350  Coast Shop        5       318  raft            40        $6
     360  Coast Shop        5       318  snorkel         10       $15
     370  Coast Shop       12       213  raft            10        $7
     380  Coast Shop       14       417  windsurfer       1    $1,325
     390  Del Mar           3       417  flippers        30       $18
     400  Del Mar           3       417  kayak            3      $230
     410  Del Mar           8       417  raft            40        $6
     420  Del Mar          11       417  raft            15        $7
     430  Del Mar          11       417  snorkel         10       $15
     440  Del Mar          11       417  flippers        20       $19
     450  New Waves         3       215  flippers         5       $20
     460  New Waves         3       215  flippers        10       $20
     470  New Waves         6       213  snorkel         15       $15
     480  New Waves         6       213  surfboard        4      $735
     490  New Waves         6       213  snorkel         10       $15
     500  Surf Mart       101       417  snorkel         20       $14
     510  Surf Mart       101       417  surfboard        2      $740
     520  Surf Mart       101       417  snorkel         12       $15
     530  Surf Mart       118       318  flippers        15       $19
     540  Surf Mart       118       318  raft            30        $6
     550  Surf Mart       118       318  snorkel         10       $15
     560  Surf Mart       127       314  flippers        25       $19
     570  Surf Mart       127       314  surfboard        3      $740
```

Appendix **2** SQL Procedure and the ANSI Standard for SQL™

Introduction *189*

SQL Procedure Enhancements *190*
   Reserved Words 190
   Column Modifiers 190
   Alternate Collating Sequences 190
   ORDER BY Clause in a View Definition 190
   In-Line Views 191
   Outer Joins 191
   Arithmetic Operators 191
   Orthogonal Expressions 191
   Set Operators 191
   Statistical Functions 191
   SAS System Functions 192

SQL Procedure Omissions *192*
   Identifiers and Naming Conventions 192
   Rollback Statement 192
   Granting User Privileges 192
   Three-Valued Logic 192
   Embedded SQL 192
   Updating Views 192
   UNIQUE Constraint 193

Introduction

The SQL procedure follows most of the guidelines set by the American National Standards Institute (ANSI) in its implementation of SQL. However, it is not fully compliant with the current ANSI Standard for SQL.* The SQL research project at SAS Institute has focused primarily on the expressive power of SQL as a query language. Consequently, some of the database features of the SQL language have not yet been implemented in the SAS System. They will be addressed in the future.

This chapter describes enhancements to SQL that SAS Institute has made through the SQL procedure. The ways in which the SQL procedure differs from the current ANSI Standard for SQL are then listed.

---

* For citations of the current ANSI Standard for SQL and the proposed draft of the ANSI Standard for SQL2, see "Bibliography."

SQL Procedure Enhancements

The query-expression has been enhanced to give it more expressive power. Most of the enhancements described here are required by the draft ANSI Standard for SQL2. The Standard for SQL2 is currently being decided upon and is expected to be the next approved standard version of the language.

Reserved Words

The SQL procedure reserves very few keywords and then only in certain contexts. The ANSI Standard reserves all SQL keywords in all contexts. According to the Standard, for example, you cannot have a column named GROUP because of the keywords GROUP BY.

The following words are reserved in the SQL procedure:

□ The keyword CASE is always reserved, and its use in the CASE expression (an SQL2 feature) precludes its use as a column name.

  If you have a column named CASE in a table and you want to code a PROC SQL statement for it, you can use the SAS data set option RENAME= to rename that column for the duration of the query.

□ The keywords AS, ON, FULL, JOIN, LEFT, FROM, WHEN, WHERE, ORDER, GROUP, RIGHT, INNER, OUTER, UNION, EXCEPT, HAVING, and INTERSECT cannot be used for table aliases. These keywords all introduce clauses that appear after a table name. Since the alias is optional, the SQL procedure deals with this ambiguity by assuming that any one of these words introduces the corresponding clause and is not the alias.

□ The keyword USER is reserved for the current userid. If you have a column named USER in a table and you want to code a PROC SQL statement for it, you can use the SAS data set option RENAME= to rename that column for the duration of the query.

Column Modifiers

The SQL procedure supports the SAS System's INFORMAT=, FORMAT=, and LABEL= modifiers for expressions within the SELECT clause. These modifiers control the format in which output data are displayed and labeled.

Alternate Collating Sequences

The SQL procedure allows you to specify an alternate collating (sorting) sequence to be used when you specify the ORDER BY clause. See the SORTSEQ= option described in Chapter 5, "SQL Procedure," for more information.

ORDER BY Clause in a View Definition

The SQL procedure permits you to specify an ORDER BY clause in a CREATE VIEW statement. When the view is queried, its data are always sorted according to the specified order unless a query against that view includes a different ORDER BY clause. See "Creating Views with the SQL Procedure" in Chapter 5 for more information.

In-Line Views

The ability to code nested query-expressions in the FROM clause is a requirement of the draft ANSI Standard for SQL2. The SQL procedure supports such nested coding.

Outer Joins

The ability to include columns that match and do not match in a join-expression is a requirement of the draft ANSI Standard for SQL2. The SQL procedure supports this ability.

Arithmetic Operators

The SQL procedure supports the SAS System exponentiation (**) operators and minimum (><) and maximum (<>) operators, as well as the sounds-like (=*) and CONTAINS operators, which match character strings.

Orthogonal Expressions

The SQL procedure permits the combination of comparison, Boolean, and algebraic expressions. For example, $(X=3)*7$ yields a value of 7 if X is 3 and a value of 0 otherwise because the result of the comparison is defined to be 1 or 0 (that is, true or false).

The SQL procedure permits a subquery in any expression. This feature is required by the draft ANSI Standard for SQL2. Therefore, you can have a subquery on the left side of a comparison operator in the WHERE expression.

The SQL procedure permits you to order and group by any kind of mathematical expression (except those including summary functions) using ORDER BY and GROUP BY clauses. You can also group by an expression that appears on the SELECT clause by using the integer that represents the expression's ordinal position in the SELECT clause. You are not required to select the expression by which you are grouping or ordering. See "order-by-item" and "group-by-item" in Chapter 5 for more information.

Set Operators

The set operators UNION, INTERSECT, and EXCEPT are required by the draft ANSI Standard for SQL2. The SQL procedure provides these operators plus the OUTER UNION operator.

The draft ANSI Standard also requires that the tables being operated upon all have the same number of columns with matching data types. The SQL procedure works on tables that have the same number of columns and on those that do not, by creating virtual columns so that a query can evaluate correctly. See "query-expression" in Chapter 5 for more information on set operations.

Statistical Functions

The SQL procedure supports many more summary functions than required by the ANSI Standard for SQL.

The SQL procedure supports the remerging of summary function results into the table's original data. For example, computing the percentage of total is achieved with $x/\text{SUM}(x)$ in the SQL procedure. See "summary-function" in Chapter 5 for more information on the available summary functions and remerging data.

SAS System Functions

The SQL procedure supports all the functions available to the SAS DATA step, except for LAG, DIF, and SOUND. Other SQL databases support their own set of functions.

SQL Procedure Omissions

This section lists ways in which the SQL procedure differs from the ANSI Standard for SQL.

Identifiers and Naming Conventions

In the SAS System, table names, column names, and aliases are limited to eight characters and are not case-sensitive. The ANSI Standard for SQL allows longer names.

Rollback Statement

The ROLLBACK statement is not currently supported. While this statement is a major SQL feature, the underlying base SAS software currently has no provision to handle it.

Granting User Privileges

The GRANT statement, PRIVILEGES keyword, and authorization-identifier features of SQL are not supported. Users may want to use host-system-specific means of security until the SQL procedure can support these SQL features.

Three-Valued Logic

ANSI-compatible SQL has three-valued logic, that is, special cases for handling comparisons involving NULL values. Any value compared with a NULL value evaluates to NULL.

The SQL procedure follows the SAS System convention for handling missing values: when numeric NULL values are compared to non-NULL numbers, the NULL values are less than or smaller than all the non-NULL values; when character NULL values are compared to non-NULL characters, the character NULL values are treated as a string of blanks.

Embedded SQL

Currently there is no provision for embedding PROC SQL statements in other SAS programming environments, such as the DATA step or SAS/IML software.

Updating Views

PROC SQL views are read-only entities in the current implementation of the SQL procedure.

SAS/ACCESS views can be referenced by the SQL procedure to update their underlying DBMS tables and views. See references to SAS/ACCESS views elsewhere in this book.

UNIQUE Constraint

The UNIQUE constraint is not supported directly in the CREATE TABLE statement. You can achieve its effect by defining a unique index on the column over which you want to enforce the unique property. The SAS System ensures that all changes to the table--even those from other SAS procedures--do not violate the unique constraint.

Glossary

This glossary defines commonly used SQL and SAS System terms and concepts.

access descriptor
a SAS/ACCESS file that describes a table or view managed by a database management system to the SAS System.

batch mode
a method of executing SAS programs in which you prepare a file containing SAS statements, or job control statements, and any necessary operating system commands, and submit the program to the computer's batch queue. While the program executes, control of the SAS System returns to the user. Batch mode is sometimes referred to as running in the *background*. The job output can be written to files or printed on an output device.

browsing data
the process of viewing a file one row at a time or a full window at a time. You cannot update data while browsing them.

column
a vertical component of a table that can contain data of a specific type and with certain attributes. A column is analogous to a variable in SAS data set terminology.

column alias
a temporary, alternate name for a column. Aliases are optionally specified in the SELECT clause to name or rename columns. An alias is one word long. The keyword AS is required with a column alias.

data type
an SQL attribute of every column in a table. It is analogous to the SAS variable attribute: type.

data value
a character or numeric value that is stored in one column in a row, that is, the intersection of a column (vertical component) and a row (horizontal component). It refers to the actual data in a SAS data file, such as the name `Smith` for the column LASTNAME.

database
an organized collection of related data. In IBM's product DB2, for example, a database is a named object that includes tables, views, and indexes.

database management system (DBMS)
an integrated software package that allows you to create and manipulate data in the form of databases. See also the entry for relational database management system.

editing data
the process of viewing a file one row at a time or a full window at a time with the intention of changing it.

engine

a set of routines the SAS System uses for accessing files in a SAS data library. Each engine allows the SAS System to access files with a particular format. The SQL procedure uses the V606 engine.

equijoin

a kind of join. When two tables are joined, for example, the value of a column in the first table must equal the value of the column in the second table in an sql-expression.

external files

files not maintained by the SAS System from which you can read data or to which you can route output.

file

a collection of related records treated as a unit. SAS files are processed and controlled through the SAS System and are stored in a SAS data library.

format, variable

a pattern the SAS System uses to display each character or numeric data value in a variable. In the SQL procedure, the default format for values in numeric variables is BEST8.3. For values in character variables, $w.$ is the default format.

full-screen procedure

a procedure that uses windows and menus to accomplish a SAS System task. For example, ACCESS, FSVIEW, and DBLOAD are full-screen procedures.

index

in the SAS System, a SAS file associated with a SAS data file that enables access to rows by index value. Having columns indexed usually makes file processing faster, although the SAS System determines the most efficient way to process data in SAS programs. The purpose of SAS indexes is to optimize WHERE-clause processing and facilitate BY-group processing.

in-line view

a query-expression that is nested in the FROM clause. It can take a table alias but cannot be named permanently. It can only be referenced in the query (or statement) in which it is defined.

interactive line mode

an execution mode where program statements are entered at the SAS session prompt. Procedure output and informative messages are returned directly to your monitor's display.

interface view engine

an engine that manipulates and processes files other than SAS files as if they were SAS data sets. The interface view engine is one part of the SAS/ACCESS software.

join

the combination of data from two or more tables (or SAS data views) to produce a single result table. A traditional or *inner join* returns a result table for all the rows in a table that have one or more matching rows in the other table(s), as specified by the sql-expression. See also the entry for outer join.

libref

a temporary name that points to a SAS data library. The default name is WORK. Librefs can be created using the SAS LIBNAME statement; for this reason, they are sometimes referred to as *libnames*.

A SAS file's complete name consists of two words separated by a period. The libref is the first word and indicates the data library; the second word is the specific SAS file in the library. For example, in SQL.NEWBDAY, SQL is the libref and tells SAS where to look to find the file NEWBDAY.

member

a SAS file in a SAS data library.

member type

a SAS name that identifies the kind of information stored in a file. The SAS System assigns the name as part of a SAS filename, such as SQL.EMPLOYEE.DATA for the Employee table used in the examples in this book. In Version 6 of the SAS System, SAS data files are of member type DATA; PROC SQL views and SAS/ACCESS views are of member type VIEW.

missing value

a value in the SAS System indicating that no data are stored in the column for the current row. The SAS System represents a missing numeric value with a single period and a missing character value by a blank space, by default. A missing value is equivalent to an SQL NULL value.

native SAS engines

engines that access forms of SAS files created and processed only by the SAS System. Two types of native engines are the V606 engine and the compatibility engine. The V606 engine is the default access method for a given release of the SAS System, and the compatibility engine accesses SAS data sets created under earlier releases of the SAS System.

NULL value

an SQL value that means the absence of information. It is analogous to the SAS System's missing value.

observation

the horizontal component of a SAS data set. It is a collection of data values associated with a single entity, such as a customer or state. Each observation contains one data value for each variable in the data set. An observation is analogous to a row in an SQL table. Observations in a SAS data set have an inherent order.

outer join

inner joins that are augmented with rows that did not match with any row from the other table(s) in the join. Outer joins are of three kinds: left, right, and full. See also the entry for join.

query-expression (query)

a table-expression or multiple table-expressions that can be linked with set operators. The primary purpose of a query-expression is to retrieve data from tables, PROC SQL views, or SAS/ACCESS views. The SELECT statement is contained in a query-expression.

relational database management system

a database management system that organizes and accesses data according to relationships between data items. DB2 is a relational database management system.

row

the horizontal component of an SQL table. It is analogous to a SAS observation. Rows in traditional SQL tables have no inherent order.

SAS/ACCESS software

a software interface that makes data from an external database management system (DBMS) directly available to the SAS System and SAS System data directly available to a DBMS. A SAS/ACCESS interface consists of three parts: the ACCESS procedure, which defines descriptor files; the interface view engine, which allows you to use DBMS data in SAS programs in much the same way you would use data stored in SAS data files; and the DBLOAD procedure, which enables you to create and load DBMS tables using data from SAS data files and PROC SQL views.

SAS data file

one of the formats of a SAS data set implemented in Version 6 of the SAS System. A data file contains both the data values and the descriptor information associated with the data, such as the variable attributes. In previous releases of the SAS System, all SAS data sets were SAS data files. SAS data files are of member type DATA. In the SAS System, a PROC SQL table is a SAS data file.

SAS data set

a collection of information stored as a unit under the SAS System. Several SAS data sets can be stored in a SAS data library. Unlike external files, a SAS data set is processed and controlled only through the SAS System.

A SAS data set is arranged in a rectangular, two-dimensional format. Each item in a SAS data set is called a data value. Data values in a row comprise an observation, and those in a column comprise a variable. See SAS data file and SAS data view for information on how SAS data sets are implemented in Version 6 of the SAS System.

SAS data view

one of the formats of a SAS data set implemented in Version 6 of the SAS System. A data view contains only the descriptor information and other information required to retrieve the data values from other SAS files or external files. Both PROC SQL views and SAS/ACCESS views are considered SAS data views. SAS data views are of member type VIEW.

Structured Query Language (SQL)

a standardized, high-level query language used in relational database management systems to create and manipulate database management system objects. SQL is implemented by the SAS System through the SQL procedure.

subquery

a query-expression that is nested as part of another query-expression. Depending on the clause that contains it, a subquery can return a single value or multiple values.

table

in the SAS System's SQL procedure, a SAS data file. See also the entry for SAS data file.

table alias

a temporary, alternate name for a table that is specified in the FROM clause. Table aliases are optionally used to qualify column names when tables are joined. Table aliases are always required when joining a table with itself. The keyword AS is optional when used with table aliases.

view

a definition of a virtual data set that is named and stored for later use. A view contains no data but is a definition or description of data stored elsewhere. SAS data views can be created by the ACCESS and SQL procedures. See also the entry for SAS data view.

When a SAS/ACCESS view--a view descriptor--is referenced in the SAS PRINT procedure, for example, the view reads data directly from a database management system (DBMS) table. You can reference a SAS/ACCESS view in the SQL procedure and in certain other SAS procedures to update the DBMS data described by a SAS/ACCESS view.

A view defined by the SQL procedure is a stored query-expression. At run time, a view derives data from its underlying SAS data files, other PROC SQL views, or SAS/ACCESS views. Its output table can be a subset or a superset of one or multiple underlying structures. However, in the current release, you cannot reference a PROC SQL view to update its underlying data.

view descriptor

a SAS/ACCESS file that defines a subset of database management system (DBMS) data described by an access descriptor file. The access descriptor file describes the data in a single DBMS table.

Bibliography

Introduction 201

Books 201

Periodicals 202

Introduction

The following books and periodicals describe SQL, relational database terms and concepts, and the ANSI/ISO standard for SQL. You may find it helpful to consult them for more information.

Books

Date, C.J. with Colin J. White (1988), *A Guide to DB2, Second Edition*, Reading, MA: Addison-Wesley Company.

Date, C.J. (1982), *An Introduction to Database Systems: Volume I, Third Edition*, Reading, MA: Addison-Wesley Company.

Date, C.J. (1983), *An Introduction to Database Systems: Volume II*, Reading, MA: Addison-Wesley Company.

Date, C.J. (1986), *Relational Databases: Selected Writings*, Reading, MA: Addison-Wesley Company.

Date, C.J. (1987), *A Guide to the SQL Standard*, Reading, MA: Addison-Wesley Company.

Gray, Peter (1984), *Logic, Algebra and Databases*, Chicester, West Sussex, England: John Wiley Company.

Maier, David (1983), *The Theory of Relational Databases*, Rockville, MD: Computer Science Press.

Melton, Jim, ed. (December 1988), *(ISO-ANSI Working Draft) Database Language SQL2*, ISO/IEC JTC1/SC21/WG3 N449 ANSI X3H2-88-1, International Standards Organization and American National Standards Institute.

Shaw, Phil, ed. (November 1988), *ISO-ANSI Database Language SQL*, ANSI X3.135, International Standards Organization and American National Standards Institute.

Stonebraker, Michael, ed. (1988), *Readings in Database Systems*, San Mateo, CA: Morgan Kaufmann Publishers.

Ullman, Jeffrey D. (1982), *Principles of Database Systems, Second Edition*, Rockville, MD: Computer Science Press.

Ullman, Jeffrey D. (1988), *Principles of Database and Knowledge-Base Systems, Volume I*, Rockville, MD: Computer Science Press.

Periodicals

ACM Transactions on Database Systems, ISSN 0362-5915, New York: ACM Press.

Database Programming and Design, ISSN 0895-4518, San Francisco: Miller Freeman Publications.

Data Base Advisor: The Database Management System Magazine, ISSN 0740-5220, San Diego: Data Based Solutions.

IEEE Database Engineering, Washington, DC: IEEE Computing Society.

Index

A

access descriptors 195
adding columns 95
aggregate functions
   See summary-function
aliases
   column 14–15, 127, 149–150
   table 26, **130**
ALL comparison 167
ALL keyword 64, 74, **155**
   EXCEPT operator 158
   INTERSECT operator 158–159
   query-expression 152
   set operators 152
   UNION operator 158–159
ALTER statement 41, 50–53, **95–97**, 98
   FORMAT= modifier 125
   INFORMAT= modifier 125
   LABEL= modifier 125
AND logical operator 21, 162, 163
ANSI Standard for SQL 189–193
   set operations 153
ANSI Standard for SQL2 190
ANY comparison 167
arithmetic operators 162–165
   enhancements 191
AS keyword 14
   column aliases 14–15, **149–150**
   CREATE statement **97**, 99
   object-item 149
   SELECT clause 14–15
   table aliases 130
ASC keyword
   ORDER BY clause 17–19
authorization identifier 192
AVG function 132, 136

B

batch mode 195
between-condition 22–23, **120–121**
bibliography 201–202
Boolean expressions 139, 179
browsing data 195

C

Cartesian product 26, 67, 142
case-expression **121–123**, 161
   set-clause 54, 114
CASE keyword 190
CHARACTER data type 123
COALESCE function 72–73, 161
collating sequences 91, 151, 162, 190
column aliases 14–15, 127, **149–150**, 195
   subqueries 165

column attributes 41
   changing 95–96
   setting 125–126
column-definition 123–124
   ALTER statement 95–97
   CREATE TABLE statement 98
column-modifier 125–126
   column-definition 123
   enhancements 190
   object-item 149–150
column-name 127–129
   ALTER statement 95–96
   CREATE INDEX statement 102
   from-list 130
   group-by-item 132
   INSERT statement 108
   object-item 149
   order-by-item 151–152
   sql-expression 161
columns 195
   adding 95
   altering 50–53
   attributes 41, 92–93, **95–96**
   definition 4
   dropping 95–97
   matching by names 154
   matching by ordinal position 154
   updating 53–55
   updating data 114–117
commas, SQL procedure 89
comparison operators 20, 162, 163
comparison predicates 20
compatibility engine 197
components
   PROC SQL statement 88, 118, 174
composite indexes 49, 103–104
   definition of 103
compound predicates 19, 21
conditions 21–23
   WHERE clause 19–21
constant values 161
   in-condition 139–140
   sql-expression 161
CONTAINS operator 165
CONTENTS procedure 47–48, 93, 103, 110, 124
correlated subqueries 32–33, **168**
   exists-condition 33–34
CORRESPONDING keyword 154
   OUTER UNION operator 152
   set operators 152
   UNION operator 157
COUNT function 23–24, 135, **169**, 170
CREATE INDEX statement 49–50, 70, **102–103**
CREATE statement 26, **97–104**
   FORMAT= modifier 125
   INDEX 49–50

CREATE statement (*continued*)
   INFORMAT= modifier   125
   LABEL= modifier   125
   TABLE   40–41
   VIEW   42–44
CREATE TABLE statement   40–41, **97–99**, 193
CREATE VIEW statement   42–44, **99–102**
   enhancements   190
   ORDER BY clause   100, 151
creating
   indexes   49–50, 69–70, 102–104
   sample tables with SQLUGDAT file
      185–188
   SAS data files   97–99
   tables   40–42, 97–99
   views   42–44, 99–102
CSS function   169
CV function   169

D

data files
   See SAS data files
data set options
   See SAS data set options
DATA step   6, 29
   comparing SQL procedure with   6–7
data types (SQL)   **123**, 195
data values   195
database   195
database management system (DBMS)   195
DATASETS procedure   103
date constants   123, 126
DATE data type   122
DECIMAL data type   123
DELETE statement   57, **104–105**
deleting rows   57
   using SAS/ACCESS views   104
DESC keyword
   ORDER BY clause   17–19
DESCRIBE statement   44, **105–106**
describing views   105–106
difference operator   158
displaying
   output   91
   output (SQL procedure)   89
DISTINCT keyword
   SELECT clause   34
   summary-function   170
   table-expression   175–176
DOUBLE PRECISION data type   123
DROP= data set option   41, 95, 98
DROP INDEX statement   50
DROP statement   107–108
   INDEX   50
   TABLE   42
   VIEW   45
DROP TABLE statement   42
DROP VIEW statement   45
dropping
   columns   95–96
   indexes   50, 107–108

   tables   42, 107–108
   views   45, 107–108

E

editing data   195
embedded SQL   192
engines, V606   103, 196
equijoins   67, **142**, 196
error checking   36–37
error codes   119
ERRORSTOP option   89–90
evaluating subqueries   31–35
EXCEPT set operator   65–66, **158**
EXEC option   90
exists-condition   33–34, **129–130**, 166
expressions   161
   See also sql-expression
external files   196

F

FEEDBACK option   14, 44, **90**, 105
files   196
first-level names
   See librefs
FLOAT data type   123
FORMAT= modifier   42, **125**, 128
format, variable   196
formats   42, 101, **125–126**, 149
   for DATE data type   123
four-way joins   66–69, 72–73
FREQ function   23, **169**
FROM clause   130, 170, **175**
   SELECT statement   16
from-list   130–132
   joined-table   142
   table-expression   175
FSEDIT procedure   100
FULL JOIN keyword   142, 146
full outer joins   72–73, **146**
full-screen procedures   196
function-call
   sql-expression   161
functions   161
   enhancements   192
   SQL procedure   169–174

G

GRANT statement   192
granting user privileges   192
GROUP BY clause   17, 23, **132–134**, 175
   LABEL= modifier   125
   SELECT statement   17, 24, 45
   summary-function   172
group-by-item   132–134
   summary-function   132–133
   table-expression   175

H

HAVING clause **134–137**, 175
having-expression 63–64, **134–137**
  remerging 134
  SELECT statement 23–24
  summary-function 172
  table-expression 175
host-variable 137–138
  references 137–138
  table-expression 175–176

I

identifiers 192
IFNULL function 161
IN clause 139, 166
in-condition 22, **139–140**
  subqueries 31, 166
in-line views 45–46, 63–64, **130–131**, 196
  enhancements 191
  joined-table 142
indexes **102–104**, 107–108, 196
  ALTER statement 96
  composite 49, 103
  creating 49–50, 102
  defining 49
  dropping 50, 107
  improving performance with 69–71, 74
  INSERT statement 109
  listing with CONTENTS procedure 103
  simple 49, 103
  unique 49–50
  UNIQUE keyword 193
  UPDATE statement 115
  using 49–50
INFORMAT= modifier 125
informats **125**, 149
  for DATE data type 123
INNER JOIN keyword 142
inner joins 143–145
inner queries
  See subqueries
INOBS= option 90
INSERT statement 26, 41, 55–57, 98,
    108–112, 159
  inserting rows 55–57
  query-expression 56–57
  set-clause 55–56
  values-clause 56
inserting rows 108–112
  using SAS/ACCESS views 108, 109
INTEGER data type 123
integer values
  group-by-item 132–133
  order-by-item 151
  ordering columns 18
interactive line mode 196
interface view engine 196
interfaces
  SQL procedure and other 78–83
intermediate tables
  See internal tables

internal tables 31, 33, 67
INTERSECT set operator 158–159
INTO clause 175
  host-variable 113, 138
is-condition 140–141
IS MISSING condition 23, **140–141**
IS NULL condition 23, **140–141**

J

join queries
  See joins
joined-table 142–147
  from-list 130
joins 26–31, 66–69, **142–147**, 197
  compared to merging 26
  complex 66
  full 72–73, 146
  inner 143–145
  left 71–72, 145
  more than two tables 30–31, 146–147
  outer 71–73, **145–146**
  qualifying columns 25
  reflexive 29
  right 145–146
  table with itself 29–30, 143
  two tables 24–25
  using indexes 102
  when to use 35–36

K

KEEP= data set option 92
keywords, enhancements to 190

L

LABEL= data set option 93
LABEL= modifier **125–126**, 128, 134, 150
labels **125**, 149
LEFT JOIN keyword **142**, 145
left outer joins 71–72, **145**
LENGTH SAS statement 123
LIBNAME statement 197
libnames 197
librefs 4, 13, 98, **177**, 197
  and tables 98, 177
  and views 100–101
  FROM clause 16
  in from-list 176
  permanent tables 41–42
  permanent views 43–44
  qualifying table names 16
LIKE clause 147
  CREATE statement 40–41
  CREATE TABLE statement 98
like-condition 21–22, **147–149**
listing indexes
  with CONTENTS procedure 110
literals 161–162

logical operators 21, 162
  order of evaluation 162
LOOPS option 119
LOOPS= option 90

M

macro facility 37, 118–120, 137
  interface 81–82
  with host-variable 137–138
macro names 137
macro variables 37, 81–82, **118–120**
  SQLOBS 119
  SQLOOPS 119
  SQLRC 36–37, 119
matching
  columns by names 154
  columns by ordinal position 154
  patterns 147–149
MAX function 169
MEAN function 169
MEANS procedure 171
member types 197
members 197
merging tables 26–31
MIN function 169
MISSING keyword 23
missing values 23, 108, **140–141**, 197
  order of evaluation **141**, 162, 163
  sorting order 18

N

N function 23, **169**
names
  in SAS System 192
  in SQL 192
native SAS engines 197
NMISS function **169**, 170
NOERRORSTOP option 89
NOEXEC option 90
NOFEEDBACK option 90
NONUMBER option 91
NOPRINT option 81, 91
NOSTIMER option 91
NOT EXISTS condition 33, 34
NOT IN condition 32
NOT logical operator 21, 120, 162, 163
NULL keyword 23
null values 140–141, 192, 197
  order of evaluation 140, 162
NUMBER option 14, 58, 91
NUMERIC data type 123
  default 51

O

object-clause
  See object-item

object-item 149–150
  SELECT clause 12
  table-expression 175
  with summary-function 172
observations 197
ON clause 71–72, **142–146**
  See also joined-table
ON keyword 142–146
  joined-table 142
operators 162–163
  See also sql-expression
  differences among systems 164
  table of 163
optimizing 74–76
  in-line views 75
  indexes 74
  joins 75
  leaving off ORDER BY 151
  omitting ORDER BY clause 75–76
  outer joins 75
  set operators 74
  subqueries 75
  summary-function 171
options 57–58
  RESET statement 89–92
  resetting 57–58
  SAS data set options 92–95
  SQL procedure 89–92
OPTIONS SAS system option 79
OR logical operator 21, 162, 163
ORDER BY clause 17–19, 133, **151–152**
  aliases in 15
  CREATE VIEW statement 100
  enhancements to views 190
  integers for ordering columns 18
  LABEL= modifier 125
  multiple values 28–29
  SELECT statement 17–19
  sorting results 17–19
  SQL procedure 89
order-by-item 151–152
  CREATE VIEW statement 100, 151
  SELECT statement 112
order of evaluation 162–163
  set operators 153
ordering data 17–19
orthogonal expressions
  enhancements 191
outer joins 71–73, **145–146**, 198
  enhancements 191
  optimizing 75–76
outer queries 168
OUTER UNION set operator 156–157
OUTOBS= option 91

P

parentheses
  with operators 162
pattern-matching
  LIKE condition 21

pattern-matching characters
  percent sign (%) 21, **147–148**
  underscore (_) 22, **147–148**
percent sign (%) 21
  pattern-matching characters 21, **147–148**
performance comparisons 76–78
performance issues
  in-line views 130–131
performing joins 26–31
period (.) missing value 23
precedence
  See order of evaluation
predicates 19–20, 179
  WHERE clause 19–21
  where-expression 179–180
PRINT option 57–58, 91
PRINT procedure 13, 46, 99
  SQL procedure 89
printing
  output 91, 99
  output (SQL procedure) 89
  tables 13
PRIVILEGES keyword 192
PROC SQL statement 57
  options 89–92
  resetting options 57–58
  syntax 89
PROC SQL views
  See views
PRT function 169

Q

qualifying column names 25, **127–129**
query
  See query-expression
query-expression **152–159**, 198
  See also SELECT statement
  as views 43
  CREATE TABLE statement 98
  CREATE VIEW statement 99
  enhancements 190–192
  exists-condition 129
  from-list 130–132
  in-condition 139
  INSERT statement 56, 109
  joined-table 142
  SELECT statement 112
  set operators 64–66
  sql-expression 161, 165–167
  steps in evaluation 45–46
  VALIDATE statement 117
querying tables
  multiple 24–31
  single 12–19
quotes, using 21, 126, 148, 161

R

RANGE function 169
REAL data type 123

reflexive joins 29–30, **143**
relational database management system 198
remerging with data 60–63, **172–174**
  enhancements 191–192
  unexpected results 61
  with having-expression 134–135
RENAME= SAS data set option 190
reserved words, enhancements to 190
RESET statement 57, 77–78, 81, **89–92**
  options 89–91
  syntax 89
retrieving data 12–37, 112
return codes
  SQLOBS macro variable 119
  SQLOOPS macro variable 119
  SQLRC macro variable 36, 37, 119
RIGHT JOIN keyword 142, 145
right outer joins 145–146
ROLLBACK statement 192
rows 198
  definition 4
  deleting 57, 104
  inserting 55–57, 108–112
  specifying with having-expression 23–24
  specifying with WHERE clause 19–23
RUN statement 13

S

sample tables 12, 185–188
  creating with SQLUGDAT file 185–188
SAS/ACCESS interface **79–81**
SAS/ACCESS software 198
SAS/ACCESS views
  as SAS data views 198
  deleting rows 57, 104
  DROP statement 107
  inserting rows 55–57, 108–109
  joined-table 142
  SAS data set options 92
  SELECT statement 11–12
  SQL procedure 99–100, 104, 108–109,
    113, 115
  updating data 53–55, 100, 115
SAS/AF software 118
  SQL procedure 82–83
SAS data files 4, 7, **198**
  See also tables
  comparing SQL tables with 4
  creating 97–99
SAS data libraries 4, 6, 8, 16, 98, 177
SAS data set options **92–95**, 176–177
SAS data sets
  See SAS data files
SAS data views 11–12, 88, **198**, 199
  SELECT statement 11–12
  SQL procedure 11
SAS functions
  See functions
SAS indexes
  See indexes
SAS names
  See names

SAS procedures
  comparing SQL procedure with 6–7
  views in 46–48
SAS System
  enhancements to SQL 190–192
Screen Control Language (SCL) interface
    82–83, 118
second-level names 177
  views 100
SELECT clause 13–14, 112–114, **175**
  arithmetic expressions 15
  columns 13–14
  enhancements 191
  object-items 12
  SELECT * 14
  table-expression 175
SELECT statement 5, 6, 7, 11–36, **112–114**
  introduction 12
  querying tables 12–19, 24–31
  specifying rows 19–24
  steps in evaluation 45–46
  syntax 12
  using subqueries 31–35
  VALIDATE statement 36–37
  views 11–12
  when to use joins and subqueries 35–36
set-clause 114, **159–160**
  INSERT statement 55–56, 108–112
  UPDATE statement 114–117
set difference operator 158
set operators 64–66, **152**
  enhancements 191
  order of evaluation 153
  SELECT statement 112
SET SAS statement 156
simple indexes **49**, 103
SMALLINT data type 123
SORT procedure 18, 91
  SQL procedure 89
sorting data 17–19
  missing values 18
sorting sequences
  See collating sequences
SORTSEQ= option 18, 91, 151
  enhancements 190
sounds-like operator (=*) 164–165
SQL 199
  ANSI Standard implementation 189
  background 3–5
  basic concepts 3–5
SQL enhancements
  arithmetic operators 191
  collating sequences 190
  column-modifier 190
  functions 192
  GROUP BY clause 191
  in-line views 191
  keywords 190
  ORDER BY clause 190, 191
  orthogonal expressions 191
  outer joins 191
  remerging data 191–192
  reserved words 190

set operators 191
subqueries 191
summary-function 191
sql-expression 114, **161–168**
  between-condition 120
  case-expression 121–122
  DELETE statement 104
  group-by-item 132
  having-expression 134
  in-condition 139
  is-condition 140
  like-condition 147
  object-item 149
  order-by-item 151
  set-clause 159
  summary-function 169–170
  where-expression 179
SQL omissions
  authorization identifier 192
  embedded SQL 192
  GRANT statement 192
  names 192
  PRIVILEGES keyword 192
  ROLLBACK statement 192
  three-valued logic 192
  UNIQUE constraint 193
  updating views 192
SQL procedure 5
  advanced features 59–83
  ALTER statement 41, 50–53, **95–97**
  bibliography 201–202
  coding differences 89
  comparing with DATA step 6–7
  components of statements 118–181
  CREATE statement 40–41, 42–44, 49–50,
    97–104
  DELETE statement 57, **104–105**
  DESCRIBE statement 44, **105–106**
  DROP statement 42, 45, 50, **107–108**
  enhancements to SQL 190–192
  INSERT statement 41, 55–57, **108–112**
  interfaces 78–83
  introduction 5–8
  macro variables 118–120
  options 89–91
  overview 88
  reference guide 88–181
  RESET statement 57
  sample library 6
  SAS/ACCESS views 113
  SAS data views 11–12
  SELECT statement 11–36, 45–46, **112–114**
  specifications 88
  syntax 89
  UPDATE statement 50, 53–55, **114–117**
  VALIDATE statement 36–37, **117–118**
SQLOBS macro variable **119**, 137
SQLOOPS macro variable 119
SQLRC macro variable 36, 37, **119**
SQLUGDAT file 12
  creating sample tables 185–188
SQLUGDAT sample library 6
SQL2
  ANSI Standard implementation 190

statistical functions
  See summary-function
STD function 169
STDERR function 169
STIMER option 69, 77–78, **91**
STIMER SAS system option 69, 77–78, 91
storing
  tables 98, **177**
  views **100–101**
Structured Query Language (SQL)
  See SQL
subqueries 31–36, **165–168**, 199
  ALL comparison 167
  ANY comparison 167
  complex 63–64
  correlated 32–33, 129–130, **168–169**
  evaluating 31–35
  exists-condition 33–34
  in-condition 31–32
  nesting levels 34
  returning a single value 165
  returning multiple values 166
  when to use 35–36
SUM function 17, **169**, 171, 172, 173
  evaluating 46
summary-function 17, 23, 60–63, 132, 142,
    169–174
  enhancements 191
  GROUP BY clause 133
  non-summary expressions 172–173
  remerging data 60–63
  sql-expression 161, 172
  where-expression 170
SUMWGT function 170
SYMGET function 118
syntax checking 89–90
syntax errors 36–37

T

T function 170
table aliases 26, 127, **130**, 199
  joined-table 143
  reflexive joins 29–30
table lookups 26
table-expression 65, **175–178**
  query-expression 152–159
  SELECT statement 112–114
table-name 176–178
  ALTER statement 95
  CREATE INDEX statement 102
  CREATE TABLE statement 97
  DELETE statement 104
  DROP INDEX statement 107
  DROP TABLE statement 107
  from-list 130
  INSERT statement 108–109
  joined-table 142
  UPDATE statement 114
tables **4**, 199
  adding columns 95
  altering columns 50–53

changing column attributes 95
comparing SAS data files with 4
creating 40–42, **97–99**
deleting rows 57, 104
dropping 42, 107
dropping columns 95–97
inserting rows 55–57, 108–112
librefs 41
permanent 41, 98, 177
sample 185–188
SAS data set options 92–95, 176–177
temporary 40, 98, 177
UNIQUE constraint 193
updating data 53–55, 114–117
virtual 99
three-table joins 31
three-valued logic 192
TODAY function 102
transforming
  data 101
  statements 14
TYPE= data set option 93

U

unary operators 162
underscore (_)
  pattern-matching characters 22, 147
UNION set operator 64, **157**
UNIQUE constraint 193
unique indexes 49–50
UNIQUE keyword 103
  CREATE statement 49
UPCASE function 148
UPDATE statement 50, 53–55, **114–117**, 159
  set-clause 53–54
updating
  data 53–55
  data using SAS/ACCESS views 114–115
  tables 114
USER= data set option 177
USER keyword 161, 190
  sql-expression 161
USS function 170

V

VALIDATE statement 36–37, **117–118**
  checking syntax errors 36
  macro variables 37
validating query-expressions 117
values-clause 108–109, **178–179**
  INSERT statement 55–57, 108–109, 111,
    178
VAR function 170
VARCHAR data type 123
view descriptors 199
  See also SAS/ACCESS views
views **99–102**, 199
  advantages of 48
  as SAS data views 198

views (*continued*)
  creating 42–44, **99–102**
  current data 100
  DESCRIBE statement 105
  describing 44
  dropping 45, 107
  enhancements to ORDER BY clause 190
  in-line 45–46
  in-line in from-list 130–132
  joined-table 142
  librefs 43–44
  permanent 43–44
  processing 99–100
  restrictions on updating 43, 192
  SAS/ACCESS views 100
  SAS data set options 92, 178
  SAS procedures 7–8, 46–48
  SAS programs 48
  SELECT statement 11–12
  seven-character names 99
  temporary 42–43
virtual tables
  See views
V606 engine 197

W

when-then-else statement 121
WHERE clause 104, 114, **175**, 179–180
  See also where-expression
  SELECT statement 19–23
where-expression 142, **179–180**
  See also WHERE clause
  DELETE statement 104
  SELECT statement 19–21
  table-expression 175
  UPDATE statement 114, 115–116
WORK data library 16, **177**

Special Characters

. (period) missing value 23
_ (underscore)
  pattern-matching characters 22, 147–148
% (percent sign)
  pattern-matching characters 21, 147–148

Your Turn

If you have comments or suggestions about the SQL procedure or *SAS Guide to the SQL Procedure: Usage and Reference, Version 6, First Edition* please send them to us on a photocopy of this page.

Please return the photocopy to the Publications Division (for comments about this book) or the Technical Support Department (for suggestions about the software) at SAS Institute Inc., SAS Campus Drive, Cary, NC 27513.